Carol Kornacki's book clearly describes the pain we cause when we hurt the ones that have been there for us. It brings to light the deep wound betrayal can and does cause. If you or someone you love has suffered from the act of betrayal, this book can help provide a much needed healing. It is eye opening, heart rendering, and very moving. Once you pick it up you won't put it down until you've read the last page.

—Mary Colbert

BETRAYAL

THE DEEPEST CUT

BETRAYAL
THE DEEPEST CUT

CAROL KORNACKI

CREATION HOUSE
A STRANG COMPANY

BETRAYAL: THE DEEPEST CUT by Carol Kornacki
Published by Creation House
A Strang Company
600 Rinehart Road
Lake Mary, Florida 32746
www.creationhouse.com

Unless otherwise noted, all Scripture quotations are from the New King James Version of the Bible. Copyright © 1979, 1980, 1982 by Thomas Nelson, Inc., publishers. Used by permission.

Scripture quotations marked NIV are from the Holy Bible, New International Version of the Bible. Copyright © 1973, 1978, 1984, International Bible Society. Used by permission.

Scripture quotations marked KJV are from the King James Version of the Bible.

Cover design by Justin Evans

Library of Congress Control Number: 2007931872
International Standard Book Number: 978-1-59979-243-9
First Edition

07 08 09 10 11 — 9 8 7 6 5 4 3 2 1
Printed in the United States of America

DEDICATION

THIS BOOK IS dedicated to my daughter Marilynn, my only child, who has been an exceedingly great joy to my life.

Marilynn, I love you more than words can express. Thank you, my precious child, for your constant and devoted labor with me in the work of the gospel of Jesus Christ. Together by God's grace we have weathered severe storms and enjoyed the sunny days. Thank you for being there through it all. You, my dear one, are every mother's dream, the perfect daughter.

ACKNOWLEDGMENTS

I WOULD LIKE TO thank Linda Smith, who found me in a bar, drunk and on drugs, lost and physically dying. Her love, kindness, and sincere expression of Christ brought me to Calvary, where I found eternal life. Thank you Linda! You looked past my faults to see my needs. I am here today as a trophy of your work for Jesus Christ.

Thank you, Pastor Tommy Reid, for being my pastor. You have taught me that integrity and character are a must, and sir, you have lived as a prime example! I love you, Wanda, and Aimee so very much.

Over twenty years ago, a man named Benny Hinn instructed thousands of people in a church service to stand up and pray for a pitifully lost and dying young woman—me. That night, I was raised from death to life. I will forever be grateful for your ministry, Pastor Benny.

I want to give special thanks to Matthew (my son-in-law) who kept on me to complete this project. "Put it down on paper," he would urge me, so I have done it. This book is my first and, I pray, not the last. Thank you, Matthew, for believing that I had something to say that needed to be heard!

And last, but not least, a special thanks to Priscilla Blanks who worked with me to complete this book.

CONTENTS

FOREWORD

My dear friend Carol Kornacki, whom I have known for more than twenty years, has written this book on betrayal using many different circumstances that people experience. She herself is a survivor of some of life's most difficult challenges, as well as betrayal. However, she has not simply survived; she has come through them stronger and has allowed these challenges to make her not only a better person, but also a very effective minister. Carol now ministers with a unique passion for the hurting. I have personally witnessed the detrimental physical and emotional effects that betrayal has upon the body. Betrayal causes our stress response to become stuck, causing us to literally stew in our own stress juices. This in turn can potentially lead to a host of medical and mental illnesses. Carol shows the reader how to break free from the bondage of betrayal.

I personally want to recommend this book, especially to those who have gone through divorce as well as other traumatic experiences. It will help them to not just deal with betrayal but also overcome it.

—Don Colbert, MD
Author of *The Seven Pillars of Health*

INTRODUCTION

WEBSTER'S DICTIONARY DEFINES *betray* as "to lead astray, seduce, or deliver to an enemy, to fail or desert, (especially in a time of need), to reveal unintentionally, to disclose...a confidence, to prove false."[1] It means to victimize someone by underhandedness or to cause a person to accept what is false, especially by trickery or misrepresentation.

Betrayal is often referred to metaphorically as "the Judas kiss," to be kissed by a friend and then stabbed in the back. However, the account of Judas' betrayal of Jesus is not the only instance of betrayal described in the Bible:

There is the story of Lot's daughters, who gave their father wine to make him drunk so that he would have sexual relations with them.

Samson loved Delilah. He trusted her with the secret of his strength, but she betrayed his trust and turned him over to the enemy. It cost him his dignity and eventually his life.

Tamar was the daughter of King David. She had a brother named Amnon who had an incestuous desire for her. In order to get her into his chambers he faked sickness and requested her care. While the young girl was caring for him, he raped her.

Then there's Peter, a dear friend of our Lord's, who was identified as one of His followers when He was on trial. Instead of defending Jesus, Peter cursed, claimed he didn't know the Lord, and deserted Him.

Betrayal comes in many different forms, such as adultery, lying, gossiping, sexual abuse, breaking a confidence, abortion, letting someone down when they are depending on you, deserting someone in need, and the list goes on.

In my lifetime, I have come to know both sides of the issue. On one hand, I have dealt with the terrible guilt of knowing that I deeply wounded someone I cared about and had to live with that feeling of regret. On the other hand, I have known the bitter agony that fills you when someone you love and trust tears your heart out by breaking faith with you.

There are many people walking around today who have been beaten down and are in terrible pain brought on by betrayal. There are also those bogged down by the guilt, shame, and remorse of their own act of betrayal. Many have never been able to forgive the one who betrayed them or to forgive themselves for hurting someone they cared for. Instead, they live in unforgiveness and hate, unwilling to discuss the act of betrayal that wounded them. Some precious people suffer for years as their hearts grow cold and hard. Others have their spiritual growth daunted by the pain of this trauma.

There is a saying that goes, "Been There, Done That!" Well folks, that's me, I have been betrayed, and I have been the betrayer.

As I reflect back on my life, I certainly would have done things a lot differently. Unfortunately, I can not go back, but I can say from the bottom of my heart that I have learned from my mistakes. I would like to make a personal statement to the people that I have come to know in my lifetime: If I have ever unintentionally or intentionally betrayed you and have never had the opportunity to say this, I am deeply and regretfully sorry. Please forgive me. To those who have known me and may have betrayed me, I sincerely forgive you and love you.

Perhaps you are still suffering from the wound of a betrayal, recent or long past. It is my prayer that in these pages you can find a story that you can relate to, one that strikes a cord in your heart. After you have read the last word and lay this book aside, ask yourself, "Am I free? Have I forgiven those who have broken my heart by betraying me? What about those I have betrayed; have I forgiven myself?"

Chapter 1
BETRAYED BY ADULTERY

THE WIND AND snow whipped against the windshield as I made my way down the icy road to the women's meeting in upstate New York. It was the dead of winter, and I knew all too well how dangerous the roads could be, having lived there most of my life. When we arrived at the banquet hall my car slid over the ice into the parking lot.

My assistant, Debbie, and I made our way up the steep stairway to the hall where the meeting was being held. It was filled to overflowing with women. The ladies in charge were scurrying about looking for more chairs to accommodate the growing crowd. "There certainly are a lot more women here than I thought would venture out on a night like this," I whispered to Debbie. "I'm not surprised, Carol. This area is an Indian reservation, and these precious women need a touch from God," she replied.

The sound of chatter filled the room; there was a feeling of excitement and anticipation in the air. A tall lady approached me. "Carol, my name is Brenda," she said smiling. "We weren't so sure you would make it tonight in this snowstorm. Is there anything I can get for you before the meeting begins?" she asked. "No, I'm fine, thank you," I answered.

1

As I looked around the room, I could see that the majority of the women there were of American Indian origin. Then I noticed her; she was sitting in the rear of the room against the wall. This young woman stood out amongst the others; she had long blonde hair and eyes as blue as a morning sky. She was wearing a smart, tailored pinstriped suit. It appeared she was alone, as she wasn't mingling or speaking to anyone. "Wow," I thought, "this woman is stunning." As I was gazing at her, our eyes met, and I smiled. She smiled back before once again looking away.

A Broken Life

The music began; everyone stood and sang. Shortly after, I was introduced. I walked up to the tiny podium and placed my Bible there. My message that night was the story of my life. I had been brought up in a dysfunctional family filled with alcoholism, infidelity, and violence. As a young girl I had been sexually abused by a family acquaintance. My father was mentally ill, and we lived in fear of his behavior. I shared about my early pregnancies and the abortions that I had out of the fear of having a child, how I lived in guilt and shame for terminating a life. I told them of my journey into a life of drugs, drunkenness, and witchcraft. I became mentally ill and attempted suicide. After years of physical and mental abuse, my body gave out to a terminal liver disease and peptic bleeding ulcers. The doctors gave me no hope. I would be dead in a few short years, they said. "I didn't care if I lived or died," I told the crowd that night. "I was dead already, as far as I was concerned. To have died at that time would have been a welcomed release!"

As I was speaking, I watched the faces of the women, each one captivated by the events in my life. I saw tears in their eyes as I explained how I had searched for love in all the wrong places and how years of rejection had left scars. I shared about the guilt, shame, and hate that grew in my heart for others, as well as myself.

When I had finished telling about my broken life, I explained about the night that a young woman named Linda invited me to church. "I certainly wasn't interested in going to a church service," I said laughing, "but Linda was such a loving person that I found myself drawn to her. I walked into that church that night addicted to heroin and cocaine, dying of liver disease, and suffering from mental and emotional problems. I had tried to kill myself more than once, and I was full of hurt and bitterness." I left the church a different person. I had found love that I had never experienced before.

I continued to tell how that love went deep into my damaged heart and began a healing that would eventually change my life. I was on the road to recovery, and in a few short months I was radically different, all because of the power of God. It was nothing less than miraculous! Gone was the desire for drugs, I was healed of hepatitis B that I had contracted from shooting up with dirty needles, and the peptic ulcer was healed as well. I once heard a man say, "There is no high like the Most High!" That is so very true. My mind was restored as I began to read and meditate on the Word of God. I was changed from the inside out. The spirits that had entered me during the years of my involvement in witchcraft were no longer welcome in my life. As I was filled with God's Holy Spirit, those unclean spirits had to leave. I was set free in a way that I cannot express in words. The ladies sat there motionless and transfixed as I finished my story of God's love and power in my life.

Then I stretched out my hand and pointed my index finger upward as I cried in loud voice, "One drop—not a teaspoon or a cup, but one drop—of the blood of Jesus changed my life forever, and I have never been the same." In that very moment, the presence of the Holy Spirit filled the room. The anointing flowed in on gentle waves. "God is able to forgive the worst of all sinners," I said softly. From all parts of the room I could hear the sound of muffled sniffles and sobs.

BROKEN LIVES, BROKEN WOMEN!

I paused for a moment to pray. "Dear precious Jesus, these women are hurting," I whispered. "You are the answer to all their hurts and brokenness. Please, let my words be your words, my arms be your arms, my heart be your heart." I then invited the ladies to come up for prayer. Suddenly, there was a shuffling of chairs as the women came rushing forward to the altar. In their eyes I saw hurt, pain, and sorrow, each one with a specific need. I looked down the long line of woman gathered for prayer. The lovely blonde woman I had seen earlier wasn't there. She had remained in her seat at the back of the hall. I turned my attention to the needs of those at the altar and ministered to them for hours.

When I had finished ministering, I went over to the table to collect my belongings. It had gotten quite late and the meeting was breaking up. All around me, women were bundling up in their coats and scarves before venturing out into the cold night air. The lady in charge approached me: "Carol, God really moved tonight. I know a lot of these women, and I can tell you their lives have been touched dramatically!" I smiled and gave her a hug. About this time, my assistant walked over and handed me my coat. "We had better get a move on," she cautioned. "The snow's coming down pretty heavy, and we have a two hour ride home!"

LAST BUT NOT LEAST

As I reached into my purse for my keys, I felt a tap on my shoulder. I turned around slowly and looked up. It was she. "Carol, my name is Sarah. Can I have a moment of your time? I really need to talk to you." Her soft voice matched the lovely face. "Certainly," I said nodding, "let's sit down right here." She shook her head from side to side, "No. Can we please go somewhere where we can be alone?" I was surprised at her request, but she seemed adamant, so I obliged her.

Sarah led me down a long hallway. I assumed she knew where she was headed. She opened the door of an empty room, entered, and beckoned me to come in. It was a large banquet room. Sarah reached for a switch, but found that none of the lights worked. At the far end, there was a large window where the moonlight poured in and filled the room with a soft, silvery glow. There were chairs scattered around on the dusty hardwood floor. We stood there for a moment, neither of us speaking.

Then Sarah slipped down to the wood floor and began to sob bitterly. I was astonished! I got down beside her and tried to lift her up, but she pulled away and lay there. Then in what sounded like total despair, I heard her cry, "I am the worst! How can God forgive me for the terrible things that I have done?" I lifted her chin with my finger and looked into her eyes. They reflected pain and misery. Her blonde hair was matted on her face, wet from her tears. I gently brushed some of it away from her eyes and asked, "What is it that you have done that is so terrible?"

Sarah stood to her feet. She hastily brushed the dust off her suit from the dirty floor. I went over and pulled two of the scattered chairs together so we could sit down, she thanked me and sat beside me. Sarah took a deep breath and regained her composure. She folded her hands and placed them on her lap and told me the following story.

AN INCREDIBLE CONFESSION

"My husband Jesse and I have been married for six years. We have a little girl that is three years old. Her name is Jade. After our daughter was born, Jesse got a big promotion at his job, and he started to make a lot of money. We bought a beautiful new home, all new furniture, and he even bought me a brand new Jaguar. Everything seemed just wonderful. Our life was like a storybook. However, as the income increased, so did the demands on Jesse. He began to work sixty hours a week. I tried to occupy my time with raising my little girl, but I missed my husband and the time we had spent together as a family. When I complained, Jesse said I didn't understand the heavy pace with which he had to keep up."

Sarah paused for a moment, reached into her purse and pulled out a hair clip. With one hand she twisted her long hair into a knot and pinned it up. She got out a tissue and began to pat her face, wiping off the tears and streaked makeup. When she had placed the tissue back into her purse she smiled at me and continued, "When the traveling started, Jesse had to go out of town at least twice a month. I knew it was important for the business, but I was becoming increasingly lonely, and it seemed we were slowly drifting apart."

Sarah stared down at her hands, as if to avoid my eyes. I sensed the next part of her story was hard for her, and the reason we had to be completely alone. "My husband has a best friend named Rick. They have been like brothers since they were kids. When Jesse started to go out of town a lot, Rick began coming over to keep me company."

I could tell that she was embarrassed as she proceeded to tell me about her relationship with her husband's best friend. "It started out so innocently, Carol. We never meant for anything to happen. I just felt so alone and neglected." Sarah twisted her wedding band as she went on. "One night Jesse was in Chicago for a business conference. Rick came over after he finished work and we had dinner. Later, after I had put Jade to bed, we sat in the living room and watched television. It was getting late and Rick had to work in the morning, so I walked him to the door to say goodnight and lock up."

"It happened while we were standing there. Our eyes met, and suddenly we were in each other's arms, kissing passionately." Sarah looked at me to see my expression. I had no intention of being judgmental and I told her so. She continued, "We went back into the living room and sat on the couch. The kissing started up again, and the passion was mounting. We knew where it was heading, but we just gave in. That night we had sex. After that we stole every moment we possibly could to be together. We just couldn't keep our hands off each other. I found myself waiting for my husband to go out of town so that I could be with Rick."

Her voice rose to a shrill, "We both felt guilty, but we were trapped in the lust and need for each other. It was out of control, and the affair went on for eight months. My husband never suspected anything. Rick was his friend, and he could trust him, he thought!"

A RUDE AWAKENING

I glanced down at my watch and saw that it was getting quite late, but felt like that moment was crucial to this woman's life. How could I interrupt or draw attention to the time?

Sarah told me that during this time she became pregnant. "When I informed Rick about my pregnancy, he was scared to death!" she said. "He came over one morning after thinking about it and asked me point blank, 'You don't think it's mine, do you Sarah? After all, you've been with both of us, right?'" I told him that I had no way of knowing. A look of disgust came over Sarah's beautiful face. "You know, Carol," she said, "suddenly the whole affair took on a different feeling. Standing before me was this man that I was sure I was madly in love with. He swore he loved me as well. A few days before, we were in each others arms, swearing devotion to one another, and now he's running scared." Sarah threw back her head and laughed weakly. Then her eyes looked deep into mine as she said, "At that moment I began to feel dirty. Things didn't look as beautiful as they had in previous months. In fact, they were starting to look just plain ugly!"

Then she said something that I have heard people say over and over again when caught in the throws of adultery. "You know, it's ironic: one moment you're in love and nothing matters. You cast all your common sense, morals, and marriage to the wind. Even the thought of your children doesn't change the need inside that is controlling you and driving you to the arms of your lover. Passion is a force, a hypnotic feeling that comes over you, and you start taking all kinds of crazy chances. Then the inevitable happens—you wake up one day and reality hits you. You begin to realize that the whole thing was based on lies, lust, and fleeting, empty promises. The laughter you shared turns to shame, regret, and sorrow. I'll tell you what," Sarah continued, as she smiled smugly, "that affair fizzled pretty quick after I told Rick I was pregnant. What had been flaming passion turned into a fear of being discovered." Sarah said that Rick lived in constant torment. Finally, he requested a job transfer to Montana, and it was granted. One night, unexpectedly, he came over to break the news to Jesse and Sarah. Jesse was crushed that his best buddy was relocating. "Why are you moving so suddenly and so far away?" Jesse asked sadly. Rick avoided his friend's eyes as he answered, " I guess I just need a change, old buddy." Three weeks later Rick was gone. "I never saw him again," she said.

"Now life was different," Sarah said with a sigh. "For a year I had been living a life of deceit, and now I had to try to pretend that everything was normal. How could I have told my husband that I had an affair, and that the child I was carrying might belong to his best friend? It was too much; I just couldn't bear the thought of hurting Jesse. So I lived in silent agony, keeping this secret to myself."

"A SON! JUST WHAT I ALWAYS WANTED"

Sarah paused, took a deep breath, and then went on. "Finally, I told Jesse that I was pregnant. He was elated! He put his arms around me and began to cry with joy. He told me he hoped it was a boy. 'This is the best news, Sarah. I'm so happy!'"

Sarah stood up and walked over to the window. Tears of sorrow and regret began to slip down her cheeks. Reliving this whole thing was agonizing for her. In a few moments she turned around and to face me once again and proceeded to tell me the rest of her story.

"Three days before Easter my son David was born, but there were problems. His little body was twisted, and his legs

9

were deformed. The doctors were baffled. They told us that it was a rare disorder, possibly genetic. As the parents, we were questioned about our families' medical histories. Jesse was puzzled and told the medical team that there was no such problem in his family or mine."

I looked at Sarah's hands, which had begun to shake uncontrollably. She had a look of terror on her face. "Now the doctors have started talking about doing a series of tests that include a DNA test, Carol," she said in a choked whisper.

She put her hand to her mouth, "What if David is not my husband's child and he finds out about Rick?" Now her whole body was trembling. "Oh God," she cried. "At times I just want to run away and never come back, but I know I can't." Her beautiful young face was filled with anguish. "As for Jesse, every night he sits at the baby's crib and prays, weeping before the Lord for a miracle for his little son!" Sarah threw her hands up in a gesture of helplessness. "It's just terrible, Carol. This whole thing is destroying me, and the guilt and shame is more then I can bare."

THE GREAT COST

I walked over to the window where she was standing and put my arm around her shoulder in an effort to comfort her. There was a long moment of silence. I looked out the window at the breathtaking winter scene. There were big, white snowflakes falling gently on the banks of the river that flowed beside the building. The branches of the tall pine trees were laden with snow, their pointed tops reaching toward the clouded night sky. There was a doe with her fawn at the edge of the river. She moved into the woods for the night, her fawn following close behind her. It was peaceful and tranquil outside, a harsh contrast with the brutal reality within these walls.

Then Sarah turned to me and whispered," Carol, what am I going to do? How can I live with myself? I have betrayed my husband with his best friend. And what about my precious little boy?"

I reached over and took her hand in mine. It was almost as cold as the icicles that hung on the windowsill outside. Up to this moment, Sarah hadn't confided in anyone about this, I was the first to hear of the guilt she had been carrying around for a long time. Suddenly in the quiet of that moment, it happened. Her chest heaved, and sobs of pain and brokenness came pouring out like a river. Sarah's body was hunched over, and she was holding her stomach, the front of her suit wet from the consent flow of tears. I walked her over to a chair and helped her sit down. We wept together.

On that cold winter night, I prayed for Sarah fervently. I knew that there was only one answer: she had to confess to Jesse about her affair with Rick and ask him to forgive her. I also knew that it was probably going to be the hardest thing she ever had to do. Still, I sincerely believed that the truth would set Sarah free. Any other way would cost her even more.

The ride home that evening was rough. The snow was coming down heavy and visibility was close to zero. Several times I pulled over to the side of the road to get my bearings. But it wasn't the treacherous road that was occupying my thoughts that night. It was the picture of that beautiful young woman named Sarah, who for a time had yielded to the temptation of adultery and now was paying a terribly high price.

SWEET TO THE TASTE, BITTER TO THE BELLY

Drink water from your own cistern, And running water from your own well.

—Proverbs 5:15

There are several different excuses that fill the path people take on their way to the sin of adultery. In Sarah's case, she felt neglected and lonely. Other couples say that they married too young or too soon and complain that they didn't know what the person was like until it was too late. For some, the romance seems to have seeped out of the relationship, and now the wife or husband searches elsewhere for the rush of passion. Television and movies portray affairs as thrilling. Everyone should have at least one, sometime. That is such misguided information.

The workplace is a prime breeding ground for relationships that can develop into full-fledged affairs. People who work closely on a daily basis may begin to share a lunch or a late evening at the office where they are alone. Then a deeper, more intimate relationship begins to develop as they discover they have a lot in common, and suddenly the sparks begin to fly. After an exchange of compliments—"I love that cologne you're wearing," she tells him—the once-benign conversations become more personal. He may complain that his wife doesn't take an interest in his career or that she has become a nag. (Of course, he doesn't include the fact that he leaves his socks in the middle of the living room or that he hasn't mowed the lawn in a month.) She may bellyache that her husband doesn't understand her and never compliments her anymore. (She fails to mention that she hasn't cooked a meal in weeks or that she doesn't want to be intimate anymore.)

The rendezvous begins with romantic dinners in out-of-the-way places, and soon they are lying to their spouses about the late nights. The first lie may be hard, but then deception becomes more frequent and a lot easier. At home there is a change in their personalities. The relationship has all the ingredients for an affair, and it is headed right that way.

Forbidden fruit tastes so good in the beginning. The sneaking around and tempting fate has a sense of intrigue to the lovers. There's the newness of the romance and the heated passions. It's all tantalizing to the flesh. Reasoning has no place here, and passion is at an all time high. It's amazing, nothing matters, and the temperature is rising. Who wants to hear it's wrong and dangerous, or that it has its pitfalls? The fruit that tastes deceitfully sweet in the beginning can make the belly feel rotten later.

People who are engaged in an adulterous affair don't take into consideration that the married person that they are sleeping with belongs to someone else. This is literally stealing someone else's property. I know a woman who had an affair with a married man. He divorced his wife to marry her. One afternoon she and I were having lunch. I told her the following, "You may be the one married to him now, but you stole him. When you steal something, it never really belongs to you. Even though you may have it in your possession, it's still stolen property!"

THE KNIFE IN MY HEART

I remember the day my husband of twenty years told me that he had been having an affair and that he no longer loved me. That day is etched in my mind clearly. He had been acting strangely for a few months. I wasn't sure what was ailing him; when I inquired he simply said, "It's between me and God. Don't worry about it!" I tried to do everything I could to make life easier and more pleasant for him. I was never suspicious, nor did the thought that he was being unfaithful ever cross my mind.

Then when I least expected it, he told me that there was another woman in his life. As I sat there listening, I felt as though each word were a knife piercing my heart. Suddenly I went numb. I tried to speak, but the words would not come out. Shock and disbelief came over me like a heavy dark blanket, as everything around me took on a surrealistic appearance. My first responses were confused questions: who, where, when, and how? All I could think of as my heart was breaking in two was, "He doesn't love me anymore." My whole world was falling apart at that moment.

A feeling of desperation came over me. I felt like I was choking. I begged him not to leave me. "I'll do anything you want, just please don't leave me. I love you, and I need you." My tears and begging only made him angrier. Holding on to his arm, I pleaded with him, but he shook me off and told me to "give it up; it's over!" I asked him to tell me what I had done so that I could change. I would change, whatever it took. "You haven't done anything," he answered. "You've been a good wife. It just happened. These things happen all the time." Shortly after that, he left for good. I can still hear the door slamming behind him. I stood there with my heart frozen in my chest. I was speechless, and I felt lost and abandoned. Immediately my life became very different.

DOWN, BUT NOT OUT!

The first month I isolated myself with my thoughts. Every day I would ask myself a thousand questions over and over again. "Was it my fault? Could I have prevented this? Why didn't I see it coming?" I went over the years of our marriage in detail trying to figure out where I had failed. At times I was sure that I would go crazy. Then a depression settled over me. Loneliness was my constant companion. I refused calls and visitors to be alone in my grief. There were times when I thought the pain would never end. I couldn't pray or read my Bible. I would lay in bed in a fetal position crying and moaning. I asked myself and God a million times why this had happened to me. "I loved him so much, I tried to be a good wife...Why? Why?" I wondered. No answer came.

It was God's continual grace that kept me from pills or alcohol. I had been delivered from these addictions at my conversion, and I am convinced God kept me from falling back into that lifestyle. There are many men and women who, when faced with the fact that their spouse has had an affair, start drinking or taking drugs. These poor souls medicate themselves in an attempt to numb the pain of losing the one they love to someone else. I thank God that this did not befall me.

I remained in a depressed state for months. I would stay in bed for days, hoping that sleep would lessen the reality of what was happening to me. When the phone rang, I'd rush to answer it. "Maybe it's him," I thought. "He's calling to tell me he's coming home." It didn't happen. I'd return to my bed of affliction and wept until I was dry. Weeks turned into months. I had lost almost twenty pounds, and the feeling that life wasn't worth living was always with me. I would cry out to God in agony, "You took my husband. Why?" The Lord would answer clearly, "I didn't take your husband. Lust took him." I knew it was true: lust destroys so many marriages, as well as the lives of those who are its victims. God tempts no one, but a person is drawn away by his or her own lusts. (See James 1:13–14.)

Then one afternoon about six months later, I had the most incredible experience. I was in the center of my living room on my hands and knees, weaving back and forth in agony. I had been crying all day. Then I heard a voice talking directly to me. It said, "I have succeeded. I have knocked you down, and eventually I will destroy you."

At that moment I realized that I was hearing the voice of the devil himself. I saw in my mind a picture of myself—broken and defeated—and it became clear to me that Satan had a plan to destroy my life. If I continued in this state, he would succeed. The ball was now in my court; was I going to let him have me? "No!" I cried audibly. "I will fight!" Suddenly, I felt the power of God go through me, and His presence filled the room. I lifted my fist and began to shake it wildly. Then I said, "You are right, devil. Look at me. You have certainly knocked me down. However, let me make myself clear: you may knock me down, but you will never, *never* knock me out!"

I knew right then that I was going to make it. I realized that though this was a terrible tragedy and I had a broken heart, Jesus had come to heal the brokenhearted and mine was no exception. I was on the road to recovery. That day I made a decision. I got up on my feet, wiped my tears, and raised my hands toward heaven. Out of my mouth poured praises to the King! I wasn't going to let Satan steal my life or the work that God had given me to do. I would take heed to fulfill the ministry to which I was called. (See Colossians 4:17.) My life would be different, yes! But my future and my happiness were not dependent on one person and what he had done to me. I had a lot to live for, and gradually things began to get better.

IT IS WELL WITH MY SOUL

A most important truth came to me: "We have a friend that feels our infirmities." He's not just aware of them, but literally feels our weaknesses and can relate to our emotions. His name is Jesus; He is the Son of God. At the lowest ebb of my life when going through this terrible nightmare, I heard His voice clearer than ever before. My friend Jesus nursed me through all the trials and tribulations and gave me strength when no one else could. He hand-picked people and sent them into my life. He gave me friends who loved and stood by me. Though in the end all things did not work out as I hoped they would, the Lord restored to me all that the cankerworm had eaten away (see Joel 2:25), and a hundred times more.

Have you had someone you love betray you by having an affair? You feel like your life is over and you can't go on. I have been where you are. I have felt your pain and loneliness. Listen, my precious friend, you can go on, and you can make it. It's not easy, I know. It will take all your strength, and it will demand solid faith. You will have to learn to stand on the Rock, which is Jesus. I have seen His power bring countless people through; these are not just words. But you must get up, get tough, and fight back. Make a decision that you will not be beaten, but you will have victory. Get your life back and your joy as well. I know it's hard to believe, but things will get better. What God has done for me, He will do for you.

I can't assure you that your spouse will return or that your marriage will be restored, but I can promise you this: Jesus Christ will never leave you or forsake you. (See Joshua 1:5.) He will be at your side walking you through whatever circumstances are before you. Even in the midst of your pain, you will be able to confess boldly for all to hear, "It is well with my soul!"

Chapter 2
BETRAYED BY ABORTION

Y OU'RE PREGNANT! THESE words can bring tremendous joy or terrible disappointment. For me, it was the latter. I was young and afraid, and I did not know what to do. The unwanted child inside of me was taking up space, and I wanted the inconvenience ended. My little girl, Marilynn, had already been taken away from me because I was a drug addict. The state had placed her in a foster home. Now I was pregnant again. I was a mess and felt trapped. My body was supposed to be a home, a safe haven for my unborn child, but my daily diet wasn't very healthy, as it consisted of drugs and very little to eat. Still, a tiny, helpless child was growing inside of me and depending on me to provide its food and safety. What I ate, it ate; what I drank, it drank.

SHOULD I RUN?

The man responsible for my pregnancy was furious. "I ain't raising no kid," he howled. "I hate kids, and I don't want to be a father!" There was no reasoning with him. He had made himself painfully clear. He didn't want a child, not now, not ever!

So one blustery October day I was dropped off at the door of the Medical Building in Buffalo, New York. In my hand I clutched two hundred dollars, the price of an abortion.

I entered the building, walked up the stairs, and went inside the office. "Sign in and find yourself a seat," a young nurse instructed me from behind a glass window. I signed the list and walked over to a chair to wait for my name to be called.

I surveyed the room, which looked like a typical doctor's office. The seats around me were filled with women of all ages. Sitting right next to me was a teenager with her mother. I assumed she was about fifteen years of age. Her mother was nervously wringing her hands and had a look of disgust on her face. She leaned over and hissed into the young girl's ear, "I can't believe you've gotten yourself into this mess. If your father finds out, he'll go ballistic. How could you be so stupid?" She picked up a magazine and began to thumb through it nervously.

In the corner across the room sat a woman who I guessed to be about forty. She was dressed in a tailored beige suit. Her nails were neatly manicured, and on her finger was a large, sparkling diamond ring. As I watched her, I couldn't help but wonder why someone with so much class would be in an abortion clinic. She glanced over at me and caught my stare, then looked away without an expression. To the left of me sat a woman in her late twenties. She had with her two small, restless children. I could see that she was at her wits end trying to keep them still. Her clothes were wrinkled and her hair was unkempt. It seemed likely that this was not her first trip to the clinic.

I placed my hand on my stomach. I knew that I had the choice to get up and walk out, but I didn't. The room emptied slowly and the wait seemed like hours. Then I heard my name called, and I walked over to the woman behind the glass window. She pointed to the door on the left and it swung open. A nurse with a stone-cold expression beckoned me to come in, and I was escorted to a room. "Take everything off and put this on," she ordered, handing me a flimsy paper gown. She grabbed the curtain and pulled it shut. "Someone will be here to counsel with you in a moment," she added. I could hear her heels clicking on the linoleum floor as she scurried away.

When I had undressed, I turned toward the wall mirror and examined my body. My belly had taken on a rounder form. I wrapped my arms tenderly around my midsection, cradling my baby. Sympathy for my unborn child was tearing at my heart. "I'm sorry, baby," I whispered, hot tears rolling down my cheeks. "I love you and want you, but no one else does," I quickly released my hands, "so you have to die." It was settled. I shook my head, trying to clear it of any further thought on the subject. I quickly changed into the blue paper gown before the nurse returned.

To my surprise, a rather pleasant woman came in. "How are you?" she asked, with a smile. "Now that's a stupid question," I thought. She handed me a pamphlet and asked, "Are you sure you want to have an abortion?" I hesitated for a moment. This was the opportunity to change my mind. I could say no and leave, but before I knew it I heard myself say, "Yes, I want an abortion." "Do you have any questions?" she inquired. "None," I said abruptly. That was it! She told me to read the pamphlet and left me in the room to wait again. That was the extent of counseling I received. Later I was handed a tiny yellow pill and a small paper cup with sip of water in it. The pill was two milligrams of Valium, a mild tranquilizer. Two milligrams of Valium in the system of a drug addict has the potency of an aspirin, but I took it anyway.

The Termination

After a short waiting period, I was escorted into a room and ordered to lie down and place my feet in the stirrups. I looked at my surroundings, which included a number of sterile gadgets and the cold-faced nurse I had seen earlier. "I just want this whole thing to be over," I thought, as fear began to grip me. Suddenly the doctor entered the room. "Good morning," he said mechanically, with no expression at all. He and the nurse made a perfect pair. It was obvious that he was there to do a job, and I guess when all you do all day is terminate life, you don't do a lot of smiling.

He did a brief examination, and then I heard him say, "Relax." Easier said than done. My breathing was shallow, and I was trembling. The nurse came over to my left side and held my arm. When I looked at her face, however, she was still expressionless, not even looking in my direction. "So much for a gesture of kindness," I thought.

I heard the hum of what sounded like a small motor and felt a tugging on my inward parts that shot up through my back. Then the humming stopped. The doctor nodded to the nurse and walked out as quickly as he had come in. I was given a few moments to relax before she helped me get off the table. I felt strangely lightheaded. I remember seeing a glass jar that was attached near the stirrups. My heart fell to my feet as I saw the blood in it. I knew exactly what it was: the remains of my unborn baby.

A few short hours before, I had come into the clinic with my body full of life and my child safe and sound inside me. Now I was leaving, my baby gone and my body empty. As I walked out into the crisp fall air, I could hear the sounds of the city all around me. My heart filled with the sense that I had betrayed my precious unborn child. My baby trusted me to keep it safe and I had deserted it. I felt lost, empty, and awkward. The procedure was over, but in years to come that day would come back to haunt me on more than one occasion.

A WOMEN'S ISSUE?

We have long made the mistake of categorizing abortion as a women's issue. The unfortunate reality, though, is that unless you had an immaculate conception, it took a man to make the child that you carried in your womb. We don't realize that men can be just as subject to the pain of abortion as women can.

I was filming a Christian television program that dealt with the issue of abortion in America. During the show, a call came in from a young Jewish man. His girlfriend had become pregnant, and he was informed after the fact that she had an abortion. He wanted the child, and was devastated that she had gone ahead with the procedure without consulting him. He felt betrayed by her. He wept as he told of the nights that he spent asking himself the same questions: What would his child have looked like? What would have been his favorite color, food, or pet? He cried as he told me the loss that he was feeling, having never held his child in his arms. A baby's life—*his* baby's life—had been cut off before it was allowed to make an entrance into this world.

THE MOURNING

I had been a Christian about six months when the memories and realization of my abortion came flooding into my mind. I was instantly confused. Had I done something that God wouldn't forgive? I was very young in the faith and knew little about the Bible.

The devil rushed in with threats and accusations. "You're a murderer," he whispered in my ear. "All the rest of your sins are easy for God to forgive, but you took the life of an unborn child."

Suddenly, I began to doubt my salvation. I started to believe a lie instead of the truth. I was filled with torment and was slowly slipping into an abyss of guilt.

My girlfriend Linda, who had been a Christian for several years, dropped by one day to visit. It was obvious as soon as I greeted her that I was not my joyful and bubbly self. After small talk and a cup of coffee at my little apartment, she asked openly, "Carol, something's wrong. What is it?" Tears welded up in my eyes and began pouring down my face. I couldn't get the words out. What would she think? "It's okay, honey. Take your time," she whispered. "I'll get some tissue." Linda returned, handed me the tissue, and sat down. I was nervous and embarrassed. "Are you ready to share with me what it is that is hurting you and stealing your joy?" my friend asked cautiously.

I got up, walked across the kitchen and grabbed the coffeepot. Without speaking, I poured us both a fresh cup to stall for time. I had a million things going through my head. Deep down I knew I could trust Linda. She had an impeccable reputation for counseling and keeping confidences. Many trusted her, and she was known for her wisdom and her love.

I sat down across from her and began to pour my heart out about the abortion. "I didn't know the terrible way they abort the children," I cried. "I was so scared, and the pregnancy was unexpected and unwanted. I never meant to harm my baby, but it seemed at the time the only way out of the dilemma." Then I put my hands to my face and just fell to pieces. "Linda, what have I done?" I moaned. "Can I ever be forgiven for such a crime?"

I put my head down and cried till it hurt. "Mourn the death of your infant," she told me. "You have a right to. Cry it out, and then we will talk about God and His grace." My knees were shaking, as the tears continued to flow for what seemed like an eternity. I had never mourned the death of my precious baby. I didn't feel like I could. But now Linda was leading me in a new path of healing, one I had never ventured down before.

Finally I lifted up my head and looked around. The sun had gone down, and the room had grown dark. "Feeling a little better now?" Linda inquired. I smiled weakly. "Yes, I believe I am ready to talk about it." This was a road that I hadn't walked before, so I treaded it slowly. Linda listened patiently without interruptions as I told her my story of how I had gotten pregnant at a young age. I had one child out of wedlock, and she had been taken away from me. It wasn't that I was abusing her; on the contrary, I was abusing myself with drugs and alcohol. When I became pregnant again I was frightened and thought that abortion was a form of birth control. So I went and had the procedure. Only afterwards did I realize that I took the life of my unborn child.

On the table in front of me was a Bible, and I leaned forward and laid my hand on it. I looked up at Linda and said, "You know, when you look at the Ten Commandments there are nine that seem forgivable. However, the one that commands us not to kill—that's a hard one. It just seems to loom out at you!" I leaned back in the chair and waited for my friend's answer, wondering if she even had one.

Linda took a moment to carefully think through what I had said and how she would answer me. Then she looked directly into my eyes. "Carol, let me tell you a story, I think it will help you."

KING DAVID'S SIN

King David ruled over Israel. During his reign he experienced terrible tragedies, some of which he brought on himself. The story of his relationship with Bathsheba in 2 Samuel 11–12 is one of them. One night the king was on the roof of his palace. While gazing out, he noticed a beautiful woman bathing. He recognized her as Bathsheba, the wife of Uriah the Hittite, one of David's most faithful men of war. Uriah was off on the battlefield defending Israel, so David secretly had Bathsheba brought to the palace and they had an affair. Later she sent word to the king that she was carrying his child. This was a sticky situation. David devised a plan to trick Bathsheba's husband into believing that the child was his. He sent orders to have Uriah brought home to his wife to create an opportunity for conception. However, the plan fell through. Uriah refused to enjoy the comforts of his wife while his comrades were at war. The king was in a predicament.

David decided there was only one thing to do: get rid of Bathsheba's husband. Uriah was sent back to the battlefield, with a letter ordering that he be sent into the heat of the battle. The command was obeyed, and David's faithful servant died by the hand of the enemy. The king had hidden his sin, so he thought!

Bathsheba was brought into the palace. She became King David's wife, and the child was born. Soon after, the baby became extremely sick. David refused to eat or drink as the child grew nearer to death. When the child died, David's advisors were reluctant to tell him for fear of what the king might do in his grief. But the king heard them whispering and in his heart knew what had happened. He got up, washed, and ate. His advisors, surprised by the change, came to him and asked, "Why is it that when the child was ill you refused food and were completely grief-stricken, but now that child has died you refresh yourself and resume your life?" David's answered this way: "When the child was sick, I prayed and hoped that he would recover. Now the child is dead. I cannot bring him back, but I can go to him someday!" (Author's paraphrase.)

Now, Be Set Free!

Linda moved closer to me and touched my hand. "You see, Carol, God is caring for your loved one. Because you have eternal life though your faith in Jesus Christ, one day you will see your baby. And know this as well," she continued, "God is a forgiving God. Before you were born, He knew every mistake you would make. Long before you knew your life, He knew you! He has given the blood of His only Son to restore you and reconcile you to Himself. Can God forgive you? He already has—two thousand years ago. If you are truly sorry and you confess your sin, He has made provision for it."

For the first time, I was able to think about my child in a new way. How wonderful to know the freedom of truth! I was being healed of the terrible guilt of having an abortion. There are times since then that I have thought of my child, but the torment is no longer there. That meeting with my gracious friend changed my life by allowing me to move past the guilt and shame into the forgiving power of the Lord Jesus Christ.

Much later, while covering the subject of abortion on my television program, I found out that there are women from all walks of life suffering from the same shame as I had. Just as there had been women of all ages and levels of the socio-economic spectrum in the clinic waiting room that day, the emotional trauma of abortion does not discriminate, but rather affects all types of women equally. In one interview, I was told that there are women in institutions that spend their days walking around clutching baby dolls because they believe that they are their aborted babies. I know of a woman who slips into depression every year around the time her aborted baby would have been born. Some women don't realize what it is that they are feeling, so they go on grieving for years without ever resolving their pain. Others feel that there is no hope, that they have committed the worst sin and God will never forgive them.

Whatever the specifics of the situation, the horrible feeling of having betrayed the unborn child threatens never to leave you. However, healing is possible through Christ. It begins by acknowledging that we have indeed sinned, then by truly repenting for that sin. When we are able to allow ourselves to grieve for our unborn child, the Holy Spirit is released in our hearts and will heal the brokenness. We must not assume any guilt after we have truly repented. He has forgiven us. We need to accept that forgiveness, accept that our child is in the care of God, and then forgive ourselves.

Chapter 3
BETRAYED BY SEXUAL ABUSE

H ER NAME WAS Michelle. She was seventeen years old when I interviewed her on my weekly television program. The subject that day was sexual abuse. This particular program meant a lot to me because as a young girl I had been sexually abused by a family acquaintance. I wanted this program to be a healing balm for people who had experienced this type of betrayal.

Michelle had come from a broken home. Her father had run off and left her mother to raise three children. Mom was lonely and desperate, and allowed her neediness to outweigh her good sense when she married the first man that proposed. Larry, Mom's new husband, turned out to be a living nightmare. He was lazy, refused to work, and drank heavily. "You go to work and I'll raise these kids right," he told her a few weeks after they were married. "I know how to make them behave, or else," he said as he balled up his fist and shook it in the air.

IN THE HANDS OF A MONSTER

Michelle told my viewers of her stepfather's cruelty: "My sister Carrie and I never knew what to expect," she said. "He would come into a room and shout, 'Get down and give me fifty pushups!'" The girls would fall down in terror and begin the routine. He would then pull up a chair and pop open a beer counting, "One, two, three. Come on girls, faster, faster." She explained, "Our arms hurt so badly that we would beg him to let us rest, but he was amused at our pain."

Larry warned the siblings that if they uttered a word he would make their lives a living nightmare. Fear of him ruled in the home. Michelle and Carrie had a little brother named Dean that was four years old. Larry hated him with a passion and would repeatedly hit the little guy on the side of the head. He was covered with small lumps. Michelle told me that she wasn't sure if her mother was aware of the punishment the children were enduring while she was at work. Though it was obvious by the bruises and welts on their bodies that the children were being subject to severe beatings, Michelle's mom never inquired, so the abuse continued. Even at school they were forced to keep up the façade. When questioned by the teachers about the bruises and fat lips, the children knew exactly how to respond: "I fell down."

Then when Michelle was nine years old, a horror began that was far worse than all the rest. One night while her mother was working, her stepfather came into her room and closed the door behind him. She told us about the terror that she felt as he began to fondle her. "I was so afraid, Carol. I just lay there because I knew what the consequences would be if I resisted. After that, it became a pattern. Mom went to work, and Larry came to my room."

Fondling later progressed to intercourse. Larry would convince Michelle that it was okay and not to tell her mom. "Your mother wouldn't understand the special love we have for each other," he told her.

Meanwhile, Michelle's sister Carrie was becoming suspicious of the time Michelle and Larry were spending alone in her room. One evening after mom had left for work, Carrie crept out of her bed, tiptoed through the house to Michelle's bedroom, and knocked on the door. As it swung open, her stepfather stood there looking down at her with his shirt opened and sweat trickling down his temple. He grabbed her by her T-shirt and asked in a drunken slur, "Just exactly who told you to come near this room?"

Carrie thought he was going to beat her, so she chose her words carefully. "Daddy, I just want you to love me like you do Michelle." Leaning against the doorframe for support, he lifted his arm and, with a sweeping gesture, beckoned her to come in. "Sure, you can come in any time," he bellowed in triumph. "It will be our little secret, just the three of us." The door slammed shut. It was the beginning of three years of sexual abuse for both of the girls.

EXPOSED

Michelle's story became even more twisted as she told of the brutality that their little brother Dean was subjected to by their stepfather. The four-year-old was put in a dark attic. He was given two canning jars— one was to urinate in, and the other jar had little pieces of bread in it. The bread was his meal for the day, and if he made any noise or wet his pants he was beaten. However, the wooden attic floors made creaking sounds that were heard below, so the small boy was often punished for just moving or shifting his little body. Such horrors did these children endure that when I met Dean he was fifteen and had spent most of his young, tender years in a detention home. He was on very strong medication and required intense counseling.

At last Michelle confided in a counselor at school. She told her about the nightmare that they were living in at home with their stepfather. When asked about her mom, Michelle simply stated, "I don't think she knows." The authorities were notified, and Larry was arrested and given thirteen years in jail. As for Mom, she swore she didn't have a hint that this man was molesting her daughters and abusing her little son.

Michelle finished her story. It took me a moment to compose myself. I leaned back in my seat and took a deep breath. "Michelle," I asked, "how do you feel about your stepfather now?" She sat up straight in her chair and looked at me with a very mature expression. "Well," she began, "forgiveness is the first step to healing. Hard as it can be, it is a must. I knew I had to face him and forgive him because Jesus has forgiven me for so much." I was stunned. She had amazed me with her sincere and loving attitude. I seized the moment, knowing this was the perfect opportunity for this young girl to reach someone who needed to hear what she had to say.

EVERY DAY

"Michelle", I said, pointing to a camera to the left of us. "Would you please look into that camera and address the people out there who have had to endure a similar violation? Speak to those who are ashamed, filled with rage toward their violator, someone whose marriage is failing, or that person who may have wondered into homosexuality or has promiscuous tendencies because they were abused as children. Would you tell them how you could forgive a man who not only stole your innocence but your sister's as well, and then tortured your little brother?"

I could feel my heart beating rapidly. Michelle had leaped over the obstacle of the wound of betrayal. I was desperate for her to touch one life with her answer.

"How, Carol?" she said, turning to look at the camera. "How do I forgive him? Every, single day. Every day! When the memories come back to torment me, when the pictures of him hovering over me come into view, when I see him taking my sisters innocence from her, and mine as well. When I think about the pain he caused my little brother, I commit myself to forgive him." Her face shined like an angel's as she continued to minister to my viewing audience. "It's like washing a wound, and forgiveness is the water; it cleans out the impurities. And then I pray for the memories to be cleansed as well."

Michelle turned toward me, and a soft smile crossed her face. "Is it easy?" She shook her head gently, "No, but I choose to get on with my life and leave those things behind me. I am determined!" Her next comment is one I will never forget: "The person who sexually abuses is not to be hated. That doesn't accomplish anything. They are to be pitied, for to abuse an innocent person is sick, and sickness needs healing."

The camera was on me; I was visibly shaken. Here was a seventeen-year-old that displayed more wisdom than people twice her age. "Let's pray," I whispered.

You're Not to Blame, and You Are Not Alone

Precious reader, if you are a victim of sexual abuse, you are innocent. You are not to blame. You have been violated, and it is not your fault. You have been betrayed, and I know from my own experience that it is difficult to try to understand why when so many questions plague us: Why me? Am I different? Did I ask for it? Could I have prevented it?

There are countless people who have come out and told their stories of sexual abuse. Support groups have been formed to encourage and help one another. Each day victims of sexual abuse are learning to walk in progressive healing, and by the grace of God and their own determination, these precious people are overcoming the pain of this betrayal.

You might ask, "How can I forgive that person or those people after what they did to me?" The answer is: by wanting to be free of the hate, resentment, and the compulsion to figure it all out. It happened; it's over. Don't give that person free rent in your mind! Evict 'em! You're right; it was terrible. I truly understand that it isn't easy to forgive, much less forget. However, easy is one thing and *possible* is another. I know it's possible to be healed and forgive because I was a victim myself.

You see, dear friend, it first takes willingness on your part. It begins with your desire to be free from the grip of feeling as though you're being taken advantage of. That process can begin for you right now if you will ask Him—Jesus—to do it. Give the pain, the humiliation, and the thoughts to Him who is able to do exceedingly abundantly above all you could ask or think. (See Ephesians 3:20.) This form of betrayal needs an exceeding and abundant power, and Jesus Christ is the Man for the job. Bow your head right now as an act of your own will. Begin to ask the Living God, who loves you and cares for you more then you will ever know, to help you to forgive that person. Yes, it's difficult and it may take time, but you are starting down the road of healing and freedom.

Trust Him today. Make the choice to forgive and to be healed. Michelle did, I did, and so can you!

Chapter 4
BETRAYED BY A BROKEN CONFIDENCE

CAROL KORNACKI IS a Christian? That is a laugh! People like her never change." That was the response of most of the people that heard about my conversion. As a matter of fact, it was the response of a friend of the family who had known me since I was fifteen years old. Steve knew me when I was addicted to drugs, involved in witchcraft, and living on the wild side. He was a close friend of the family, so he was familiar with the problems at home: the drunken parties, my father being in and out of mental institutions, and the dysfunctional aspects of our childhood. Now he was being told that I was preaching the gospel!

For those that had known me, it was hard to believe that my life could be changed. I had been pitifully addicted to drugs, and I was known to wander the streets and be jailed for my own protection. It was no surprise to me when Steve muttered, "Carol changed? Give me a break." I had to prove to my old friend that I was not the same person he used to know. God had indeed taken my old life and nailed it to the cross and given me a new life.

Steve's wife, Sherry, was a Christian. She was a wonderful person, and I liked her right off the bat. We became the very best of friends. Steve had a drinking problem, and the marriage was not doing well. He didn't want me hanging around and certainly wasn't interested in my conversion story. But his wife and I were friends, so there I was right in his home, much to his dismay!

CHANGED INTO A DIFFERENT MAN

Then it happened. Steve started to show an interest in the things of God. He began attending church, and when we least expected it, he made a decision to give his life to the Lord. In the most beautiful way, Jesus Christ came into his heart. He became a different man, and the transformation was nothing less than phenomenal. Instantly, Steve's desire for alcohol vanished, and his marriage improved.

Steve and Sherry started a Bible study in their home on Tuesday nights. They would bring in wonderful teachers and a speaker to address the growing crowds. At one particular study, they had thirty-three children in a room with a special minister to watch them and teach them about the Lord. Throughout their apartment were sixty seats filled with hungry new converts. I never saw anything like it. What began with a handful of people grew into the biggest Bible study in the city.

Drug addicts, prostitutes, alcoholics, and people of every walk of life were receiving Christ at those Bible studies. There was talk of many miracles in the meetings. Pastors in the surrounding areas would attend on Tuesday night because they heard that God was moving so incredibly. This Bible study was literally populating churches in that city.

Steve went to work every day with his Bible and loved reading it on his lunch breaks. There was no shame or embarrassment; he was honored to tell anyone about his conversion. If they asked, he would explain how wonderfully God had changed his life. He was bubbling over with excitement, and people were amazed at the boldness and beauty of his walk with the Lord. God was using him beyond his wildest dreams, and he loved every minute of it.

BETRAYAL

One day Steve decided that he wanted to talk to a counselor at the church. He was sure that a talk with someone he could trust would enable him to open up and deal with some of the guilt he was feeling from the things he had done in the past. Since these things were extremely personal, Steve wanted someone who would honor his privacy. So, he made the appointment. The day of the meeting he sat in front of the counselor and said, "What I am about to tell you is in the strictest confidence. You must promise me it will not be repeated." The response of the counselor was immediate. "You can be assured anything said here will go no further. You have my word." Steve poured his heart out. He released every intimate secret and hidden thing with complete abandonment, convinced that all he had shared would never be repeated.

About three weeks later, Steve found out that some of the church staff had become aware of the contents of his conversation with the counselor. He was crushed, torn up. He came home from church that day with a blank look on his face. "I have been betrayed," he moaned. "I trusted someone with my life and they have betrayed me. Never again," Steve said with a determination. "I will never trust anyone. If you can't trust a Christian, who can you trust?"

After that Steve began to change. The drinking started, and eventually the Bible studies ceased. He was different now, and he trusted no one. Steve made himself a promise that he would never share any of his feelings with anyone. "Why should I?" he thought. "It only leads to betrayal."

I Ain't Telling Nobody, Nothin'!

If any man among you thinks he is religious, and not
bridle his tongue but deceives his own heart, this one's
religion is useless.

—James 1:26

What is it that compels us to release secrets and break
confidences? Why do some of us lack the control that we
need at the time we are engaged in these kinds of conversations? It's like some kind of flippancy comes over us. When
someone puts their confidence in us, they are putting their
lives in our hands. They trust and depend on us not to repeat
those things. Yet, many of us do it without even thinking about
it. The things that have been entrusted to us become public
knowledge. It isn't five minutes after we have spoken that
we know that we have made a mistake. But by then it's too
late. The words are out and the damage is done; we can't take
it back. I am more than sure that at one time or another a
majority of us have done this and found ourselves regretting
our actions terribly. I know I have.

When I was on the streets, there was this saying, "The
only way to keep a secret between three people is if two of
them are dead." It certainly isn't the nicest saying, but sadly
enough at times it rings true. You give yourself to someone
by letting him or her in to your heart and revealing your
deepest secrets, and they break that confidence. The pain can
be unbearable, as in Steve's story.

I know people that feel that they can never trust again
because of incidents like the above. I remember how terribly
broken I was when this happened to me by close friends. I
was convinced I would never get over it. I did, however, and I
am glad that I faced the hurt and worked out the distrust that

I harbored. It isn't likely that I will ever share a confidence with the one that betrayed me, but I learned that I didn't have to lose faith in everyone because I had this happen to me. I have, however, become very cautious about whom I share my feelings and private life with. We should be discriminating in sharing our private matters, just as the people we open up to should be careful not to repeat that which has been entrusted to them. Proverbs remind us of this when it says, "Whoever guards his mouth and his tongue Keeps his soul from troubles" (Prov. 21:23).

IF I CAN'T TRUST ME, WHO CAN I TRUST?

I have a dear friend Conner who lives in England. He once went to God in prayer and asked, "Lord, why can't I trust anyone? Why are people so untrustworthy?" The Lord spoke to his heart and replied, "Can you trust yourself, Conner?" My friend answered honestly, "No, Lord, I can't!" The Lord's response was strangely unique: "If you can't even trust yourself, how do you expect to trust others?" It is true that placing our trust in people has become increasingly difficult because we have become careful to trust. And surely there are times when we struggle to trust ourselves as well, with the secrets of others.

The Bible says, "The heart is deceitful above all things, And desperately wicked; who can know it?" (Jer. 17:9). We must allow the Holy Spirit to go into the depths of our heart and help us to forgive and become trustworthy.

I began by asking God to forgive me for the times that I had been guilty of breaking a trust by speaking too soon or saying too much. After having done that, I decided that if it were at all possible I would make amends with the individuals I had offended. In some cases this was impossible, but in others I was able to let them know how sorry I was. Then I prayed, "Lord, put a guard at my mouth to protect my tongue from speaking evil, and keep my ears from hearing those things that will ensnare me." I then committed to forgive those who had hurt me by breaking a confidence. I wanted to put those people at liberty in my thought life and in doing so set myself free. The Lord was gracious in this matter and gave me the strength to let those issues go. I didn't feel a need to resume a relationship with the individuals involved, but I felt much better after forgiving them.

For those who have suffered this type of betrayal, I am not making light of it, and I know that betrayals that happen repeatedly can cause a lot of harm. However, it isn't fair for you to carry this burden. There is liberty and victory when we set out to forgive those who have spoken about us or revealed a secret we entrusted to them. Make a quality decision to be free. Turn your hurt into a stepping-stone to growth and learning. Let us all strive to be trustworthy, walking in the spirit and not in the flesh, and bearing the fruit of the spirit as we learn to love and be faithful to one another. Oh, what an incredible world this would be to live in if we could all learn to bury confidences in our heart, commit them to prayer, and guard our tongue!

Chapter 5
BETRAYED BY A HOMOSEXUAL AFFAIR

S HOCK TELEVISION—IT HAS drawing power and it makes big money. Surf through your channels in the afternoon and you will find talk shows that glamorize sex, violence, and, quite often, homosexual relationships. The producers will invite a couple on the show, knowing that one of the two has a secret that he or she will reveal to the other on national television. The outcome of these confrontations can lead to violent fights and unbelievably embarrassing moments. I find shows of this nature repulsive, but the people that seek momentary fame by appearing on these programs have certainly experienced what it is to be betrayed.

FIFTEEN MINUTES OF FAME
CAN CAUSE A LOT OF PAIN

One afternoon I happened upon one episode. It featured a young, attractive couple that was planning to be married in a few short months. However, they appeared as guests on this show because she wanted to reveal to him a secret. It was clear that the young man, Gary, had no earthly idea what he was in for. Perhaps he expected some wonderful surprise from Rhonda, his bride-to-be. At the opening of the show,

41

the host introduced the couple and began to ask them some questions. "So Gary, are you happy?" Gary, who appeared to be a little shyer than his girlfriend, answered, "Yes, we love each other very much." He reached over and kissed Rhonda's hand softly in a romantic gesture. The host smiled sheepishly at the audience before turning and addressing Rhonda in his most robust voice. "Now Rhonda, you have a secret that you have been keeping from Gary, right?" he asked. The pretty young woman answered shyly, "Yes, I do." The host nodded politely and said, "Go ahead and tell him. I'll leave you alone." Now mind you, my precious reader, the host walked less than ten feet away, three hundred people were watching in the live audience, and several cameras and microphones turned on the couple to catch their every word and gesture for the nationally-televised broadcast. How private was this moment supposed to be?

As Rhonda turned to face her fiancé, the camera caught a close up of Gary's puzzled face. "You know I love you," she said coyly. The audience was still. You could hear a pin drop. "But," she continued, "there is something I must tell you." At this point, Rhonda displayed a look that indicated she might be hesitant to go on. "Well, I am involved with someone else. I have been having an affair." The young man turned pale as he managed to choke out one word, "Who?" Sensing a prime opportunity for some drama, the host interjected, revving the crowd. "Well," he shouts enthusiastically, "let's meet Rhonda's lover!" Suddenly, out of the back of the stage, a blond in a short, low-cut spandex dress strutted out. On her ankle was a butterfly tattoo. She was wearing stiletto heels and a smug look on her heavily made-up face. When this girl approached the couple, Rhonda stood up to greet her. They embraced and began to kiss passionately. The crowd began to roar with excitement while Gary, ashen-faced and still sitting in the chair on stage, does a slow meltdown. This poor guy not only discovered that his fiancé had been betraying him with this other woman, but she humiliated him in front of millions of people on national TV. Oblivious to his shame, the audience was howling as they cut to a commercial. "That's TV, folks!"

Unfortunately, when the cameras turn off, lives still go on. As I sat there, all I could think about was the condition of that poor young man who was betrayed by the one that he loved. The show ended and the host and audience went home without a thought to the life of that man and the lasting scars that he may be left with.

God Built Man and Woman Different for a Reason

I cannot emphasize enough how many calls we get in our office from hurting people, some whose lives are shattered because the person they love has betrayed them with someone of the same sex.

How does one deal with the pain of losing someone you love to a homosexual relationship? Like any other betrayal, this can be painful and humiliating. Certainly, we cannot ignore the recent rise in divorce as a result of this issue. For several years people have been coming out of the closet and openly admitting to this lifestyle.

It is my opinion it was never God's plan for man to be with man or woman with woman. A simple observation of the human body makes it clear that men and women are built differently, and for a reason! The woman has a womb to bear children. The man is built to plant the seed from his body in the woman's womb to procreate. If God had other plans, I would think He would have made us differently.

I certainly do have compassion for those who are in question of their sexuality. I am not standing in judgment, nor trying to cast any slurs.

How does one deal with the pain of losing someone you love to a homosexual relationship? Some of the questions that one might ask him or herself are, Was this my fault? Did I cause my spouse to seek the affections of this person of the same sex? Have I failed them sexually? Wasn't I adequate? These questions, left unanswered, can catapult a person into a confused mental state.

The answer to the first question is no. You are not to blame! Even though there may have been a healthy sexual relationship and you had children together, and though you may never have suspected that this problem existed, it is still likely that the spouse entered into the marriage already aware of these feelings.

Oftentimes people struggling with questions about their sexuality believe that a heterosexual marriage may help to change these feelings and allow them to live a straight life. However, by ignoring their desire for the same sex rather than resolving it, they weaken and give into the temptation. Suddenly his or her unsuspecting spouse is faced with the realization that they are living with someone who is totally different than they thought. The shock of this ordeal can last a long time, but I can assure you that countless people get through it and go on with life.

I have a dear friend who was betrayed by her husband. She found out that he was having sexual relations with other men and later discovered that he had given her herpes, a sexually transmitted disease. It nearly took her out. One day at lunch she told me what a wonderful father he was to the children and how much they loved him as did she. "I never suspected he was capable of such a thing," she told me. "To my surprise, he was arrested for exposing himself and making lewd advances to an undercover officer. Then he informed me that he was in love with another man and wanted a divorce." As I listened to her story I couldn't help but recall the other incidents where this had happened. It seems that in today's society it is more prevalent. I have ministered to countless people whose marriages as well as relationships have been hurt by discoveries such as this. Betrayal in this fashion is no less painful. In some cases it seems worse.

I will not judge or condemn a person who is in question of their sexuality and married to someone. That never brings victory to a broken marriage. Truth, openness, and being willing to understand with a lot of sincere prayer will work far better.

I know of marriages that this kind of betrayal has destroyed. In the case of my friend and her husband, they divorced shortly after. Yet, she remained respectful of him when it came to the children. She was sure the whole thing had done enough damage to their hearts and minds, so she refused to be a source of more hurt. The children were confused and terrified that a divorce was in the works. It took a lot of explaining and a tremendous amount of support by friends, and of course, prayer. However, through it all she made it. God surrounded her with His love and comfort, and in the end, though the marriage ended, she remained her ex-husband's friend, and he continued to be a good father. Years later he remarried and so did she. Today my dear friend has found happiness. If you ask her if it was an easy road, she would tell you those were the darkest days of her entire life. If you asked her what it was that got her through, she would tell you without hesitation, loving when it was the most difficult, forgiving when it seemed impossible. And most of all, God's provision of strength and power.

Please Take Me Back

One question I have been asked is this, "What if my spouse asks me to forgive him (or her) and continue in the marriage?" This is a question no one can answer. There are so many different scenarios, and each person reacts differently. Some have been repulsed and totally refuse to reconcile, while others say, "I want to reconcile for the children's sake." Still others love their partner and are willing to go the extra mile to "get things back together again." I know of several marriages that have suffered this type of betrayal and today they are together as a family. The "secret" is out and the healing has begun. For some, of course, it can be the end of a marriage. The trust factor has been broken, not to mention the shock that the partner goes through. The papers are filled with stories like this of "prominent" people who are caught with someone of the same sex. The public is stunned and the embarrassment for the family is astronomical.

A Road Called Healing

This type of betrayal is becoming more prevalent in our society, so there is a serious need for support groups to cover this with their expertise and help repair broken marriages. Stay clear of condemnation or judgment; God loves the sinner and He is there to heal the brokenness and restore the marriage if they are willing to be open and honest and get the help needed. If the marriage is "repairable" and one is willing to stay the course, then there is hope. I encourage anyone who has been through this to find a good loving person to talk to, one with whom you can share your inner feelings and especially someone whom you trust to pray with you. Prayer is the key; I truly believe it is the balm that brings healing.

Unfortunately, some marriages will be beyond repair, or a partner will "want out." The road to recovery for the spouse that is betrayed can be long and hard, but there is a road called healing, and it is available to all who will yield to God for it. He can and will bring you through.

.

Chapter 6
BETRAYED BY LIES

S UZANNE IS A dear friend of mine, as well as a unique lady with a tremendous sense of insight and wisdom. I recall an interesting conversation that we had one morning. It was an unusually cold day in Florida during the month of March. We were sitting in her beautiful family room cuddled up on big comfy couches and sipping tea sweetened with honey and cream. Suzanne is from England, so we have shared many conversations over a cup of tea. That morning she had a fire going in the fireplace. We sat there silently watching the flames and listening to the wood crackle. It was warm and wonderful.

Finally Suzanne's soft voice broke the silence. She shared an experience with me about a close friend who had lied to her about some important issues. I sensed sadness in her voice as she expressed the hurt she felt because of it. "I love her and I forgive her, but as for the trust, it's gone," Suzanne said. "I can take just about anything, Carol. But a friend lying to me is something I have little tolerance for."

SHE OPENS HER MOUTH WITH WISDOM

Setting her cup on the coffee table in front of her, she leaned back on the couch, pausing for a moment to collect

49

her thoughts. "I believe when someone you trust lies to you it is a form of betrayal because you are supposed to trust that what they are saying to you is the truth. Don't you agree?" Her lovely blue eyes reflected the seriousness of her question.

I knew at that moment Suzanne was not expecting me to simply agree. She was looking for an honest answer. Someone in whom she had placed her trust had lied to her and she felt betrayed. I took a minute to think about it and decided she was right. I looked across the room to where she was seated and answered her this way: "Yes, Suzanne, when we lie to someone, we are breaking the trust factor. Therefore, it is betrayal."

Webster's dictionary defines *trust* in this way: "to rely on truthfulness or accuracy of" or "assured reliance on the character, ability, strength or truth of someone or something; one in which confidence is placed."[1]

You would have to agree that if you trust someone and they break that trust, you feel betrayed. How many of us have been guilty of betraying someone with a lie, someone who had placed confidence in us? The Word of God in Proverbs 6:17 expressly states that the Lord "hates a lying tongue." How quick we are to lie to save ourselves or to cover up a wrong we have done. Trust must be a factor in every relationship, and lying dampens the growth and progress of trust or, worse, destroys it completely.

This next story is an example of a small lie that bore a great cost.

YOUR LIPS HAVE SPOKEN LIES...

Aaron was a hard-working man, and he had a well-paying job. Still, the bills were piling up. The demands at home were rising now that their daughters were teenagers with designer taste! College was a must, so the money had to be set aside for the girls' education. Aaron was in charge of the checkbook and paying all the bills. Christy, his wife, was given a certain amount of money a week for food and extras.

There were no questions asked when it came to financial matters, like the balance in the checkbook or how things were getting paid. Aaron would tell Christy over and over, "Don't worry about it, honey. I have everything under control. The bills are being paid, so you needn't worry; trust me," and so she did. After all, Christy had no reason not to. She loved her husband, and if Aaron said everything was all right, then everything was all right.

One afternoon on a warm spring day, Christy had an experience that would forever change her life and the trust she had in Aaron. That morning as she hurriedly left the house, her mind was filled with the many things she had to get done. "I have to be home by three o'clock when the bus lets the girls off," she thought. "And of course, Aaron will be home by four o'clock, and he'll expect dinner on the table."

Christy jumped into the truck, turned on the ignition, threw it into reverse, and pulled out of her driveway. Her red SUV glistened in the afternoon sun. She turned on the radio to some easy listening tunes. "I'll stop at the grocery store and pick up some fresh salmon for dinner," she said to herself. No sooner had Christy made that decision than another pressing thought entered her head. "I've got to pay the electric bill, pick up the dry-cleaning, I need paper towels, and the deposit has to be made. I hope I'll have time," she said aloud.

Christy's late start put her right in the middle of noonday traffic. Irritated drivers were honking their horns. With car windows opened, a mix of warm spring air flowed in along with the shouts from adjacent cars, " Come on, get moving!" Christy paused at the red light and waited for it to turn green. Then placing her foot on the gas pedal, she moved forward into the intersection. Suddenly there was an impact that sounded like an explosion. She felt her car being pushed, scraping the pavement, then everything came to a dead stop. That was the last thing she remembered before everything went black.

When Christy woke up, she found herself in a strange place. She looked around; when she moved her head she felt intense pain.

Standing at the foot of the bed was a nurse in a crisp white uniform. As Christy tried to speak the nurse rushed over. "Relax, honey," she cautioned. "You've been in an accident. You shouldn't be moving around. Your husband will be here shortly." The pain seared through her body. "Am I hurt badly?" she asked, tears streaming down her face. "Not now," the nursed motioned. "Try to get some rest."

"Christy," a voice whispered. A gentle hand brushed her shoulder, but even the slightest touch sent pain through her whole body. It was Aaron. "Honey, you are going to be alright. You got pretty beat up in the accident. A young kid ran a red light and hit you broadside." Aaron's concerned expression was obvious as he leaned forward and kissed her swollen cheeks. "Just get some rest honey, please? The kids are all right and I am taking care of everything."

When Christy was released from the hospital, her recovery took six months. A private nurse was hired to care for her at home. It was a great expense, but Aaron assured her that they had the best insurance. Nothing to worry about! By the end of summer, she was starting to get around. One evening while sitting on the back porch, she turned to Aaron and asked, "Honey, how come the insurance company isn't taking care of all of these bills?" "Relax, Christy," Aaron answered abruptly. "I'll take care of it."

Wednesday morning the call came. It was the hospital inquiring about the bill. Why wasn't it paid? How were they intending to cover the cost? Christy interrupted the lady to explain, "Our insurance company will be covering all of this." The woman informed her, "I am sorry ma'am, there must be some mistake. We checked with your insurance company. They claim your insurance was terminated over a year ago." Christy let out a nervous laugh and said, "Why, that is ridiculous. My husband pays our insurance every month." The lady's reply was polite but clear: "I am very sorry ma'am. I suggest you check with the insurance company yourself."

Christy immediately began her own investigation. What she found shocked her. First of all, there was no medical insurance, as the premiums hadn't been paid for over a year. She also found out that Aaron had slipped in paying his car insurance, and as a result the SUV wasn't covered. The cards she carried were useless. Aaron had lied about paying the insurance premiums. Christy laid the phone on the receiver and sat down, dumbfounded. "Why didn't he tell me?" she asked herself. "Aaron is a liar. He can't be trusted. I'm his wife, and he lies to me!"

At four o'clock on the dot, Aaron arrived home from work. Christy was waiting at the door. "Hey honey, dinner ready?" The look on her face told him something was terribly wrong. "What's wrong? Are the kids alright?" he asked. "The girls are fine," Christy shot back, "It's us that is all wrong!" Now he was confused. Christy sat down in the living room and motioned to Aaron to sit across from her.

"Why have you been lying to me, Aaron? I talked to the insurance company today." Aaron sputtered as he tried to explain, "It's okay, Christy. The other guy is at fault and he has to pay." Christy's face dropped. "That's not the point, Aaron. You've been misleading me. I believed you when you said that you had everything under control." Suddenly Aaron became angry and retorted, "What's the big deal? It's a small matter. Why are you so mad?" Christy whirled around. "A small matter? Is lying a small matter to you? The question is, Aaron, what else have you lied about?"

Truth is a strong element in a relationship. Whether it is in a marriage, friendship, a business agreement, or even family members, there must be absolute honesty. Our word must be our bond.

THE SPIRIT OF TRUTH

Truth and trust must start at the top. Our government has been invaded for years with lies, cover-ups, and scandal. How well I remember when President Clinton came on the television with his finger pointing at us insistently, claiming that he never had sex with "that woman". Later, when he was exposed and the truth came out, he had to eat crow and admit that he had lied. Questions about truth and the nature of lying were instantly at the forefront of discussions in America. The fact is, the truth is simply truth. Any deviation from it for any reason is a lie. President Clinton remained in his position as president of the United States, but his word was no longer his bond. He put in our mind questions of his honor and integrity, and we, the American people, were left with the feeling that we were lied to, deceived, and betrayed!

"You lied to me," creates a strange atmosphere. No matter what the excuses, lying is wrong and we should avoid the dangers of it. We have accepted lying as a normal—even *necessary*—way of life. Our children hear us lying, and assume that it is acceptable. Yet when they lie to us, we go into a rage. My dear reader, that is pitiful! The truth is that if we lie, our children will lie as well. What a scary thought for their future if the world is to become a place where lying is as acceptable as brushing your teeth!

If we as believers have received the Spirit of God in our hearts, then we are filled with the Spirit of truth. This sacred Spirit does not harbor lies, nor is He the author of a lie. Jesus clearly stated that the devil is a liar and the father of lies. (See John 8:44.) When we set out to betray someone through lying, we hook up with the devil and subdue the voice of the Spirit of truth. The outcome is never good, no matter how necessary the lie may have seemed or how innocently we feel we told it.

The good news is that we can choose to make a godly commitment to hear the voice of the Holy Spirit. It will take practice, as well as determination on our part. The devil will fight us on this, and the flesh will battle against us when we are called to choose the better road, the road of truth. But know this: the outcome of truth is always victory!

GO TO THEM. GO TO GOD.

If you know in your heart that you have betrayed someone by lying to them, you have given it to prayer, and you are sure that there is a release in your spirit, then go and ask for forgiveness. How they respond to you is not the issue. It could be that they are very hurt and cannot receive your apology or extend forgiveness right then. The point is you made the effort to reconcile and ask forgiveness. Rest in that!

In some situations, it may be impossible to reach that person or persons and ask forgiveness. In that case, we can confess our sin to God our Father, and "He is faithful and just to forgive us our sins, and to cleanse us from all unrighteousness" (1 John 1:9). Once we have confessed our sin, we cannot let the enemy fill us with guilt. Know that "if our heart condemns us, God is greater than our heart" (1 John 3:20).

The Bible expressly states, "The tongue of the righteous is choice silver" (Prov. 10:20). Let us practice giving our tongues to speaking the truth and nothing but the truth, and avoid betraying people by way of lying, so help us God!

Chapter 7
BETRAYED BY GOSSIP

I REMEMBER AN EMBARRASSING experience. At the time it didn't seem a like a major incident, however, it taught me a valuable lesson. It happened during my years as a drug addict while I was working in a bar as a cocktail waitress. I did quite well at making money to support my ongoing drug and alcohol habits. I was sure I was the best waitress in the place. Whenever anyone came in who could do a better job, I became intimidated and jealous.

JEALOUSY CAN LEAD TO GOSSIP

One afternoon a new girl came on board. She was younger, prettier, and a better waitress. We became acquainted and a relationship developed. As time passed, we became friends.

One day when I was working alone, I found myself engaging in a conversation with some people at the bar. Her name came up and it was followed by some negative comments, which led to talk about her personal and private life. Suddenly, the atmosphere was charged with gossip about this "friend of mine."

Gossip is strange. You find yourself trapped in its clutches after only a few words. As I stood there with the others partaking and adding my own comments, I felt a tap on my shoulder. When I turned around, my friend was standing there. My immediate thought was, "How much did she hear? How long had she been listening?"

I was embarrassed beyond words. There was anger flashing in her eyes as she said to me loudly, "Carol, if you've got something to say about me, why don't you say it to my face and not gossip about me to the whole bar?" I lowered my head in what was one of the most embarrassing moments of my unsaved life. I'll never forget the look on her face of mixed disappointment and anger. I know how betrayed she must have felt. That night I learned a lesson about how painful gossip can be.

THE LADDER OF SUCCESS: A BREEDING GROUND FOR BETRAYAL

It wasn't too long after I had come to know the Lord that I had an incident in which I was hurt by gossip, just as I had hurt my friend in the bar. When I was just starting out in the ministry I made some wonderful friends. One day I discovered that one of these dear friends that I trusted had been working at destroying a relationship that I shared with someone else by gossiping about me. I was devastated. It threw me for a loop. "Wow," I thought, "this person cannot be trusted." Obviously he was trying to make himself look good by making me look bad. When this friend asked me to forgive him, I knew that I had to for his sake and for mine. However, his words did cause a lot of hurt, and relationships suffered for years after as a consequence of the betrayal. The whole mess would never have occurred if this individual had guarded his mouth and avoided gossip.

Why is it that we allow ourselves to be dragged into conversations that betray the people who love and trust us? Is it to obtain a position, success, or maybe a need to feel important? Do we really want to destroy one another with words that have such potency? Why is it that our flesh revels in such conversation? Many times it is to gain position or promotion.

I once heard a saying that goes like this: "Watch who you step on your way up the ladder of success; you are likely to run into them on your way down." Often times when people are striving for success, they will do and say things behind someone's back to get to the top. Unfortunately it is in these times that friends may betray friends. Someone once said, "At the end of your life if you can count your true friends on one hand, that is a lot!" That is not to imply that there are no good friends, but friends can betray one another and, when it happens, it causes a deep wound.

No words can express the hurt when someone you cherish as a friend has an agenda for advancement at your expense. One moment you are close, and then a desire for success changes their personality entirely. These people quickly forget the faithful friends who supported them and loved them in the hard times. I have ministered to countless people who have been injured by people they loved that were on their way to advancement in a job, company, sport, or even a ministry when fellow Christians betrayed them. This kind of betrayal affects people of all walks of life.

THE KING WASHED FEET

I have always thought it strange when people push and shove their way to the top of a career or ministry, leaving a pile of broken people behind them. Jesus advanced to the greatest ministry known to man, yet made no reputation for Himself. He humbled Himself unto the point of death. The night He was betrayed, Jesus took off His outer garments, wrapped Himself in a loincloth, knelt down, and washed the feet of the disciples—including the feet of Judas, who would betray Him to the enemy. (See John 13.) How can people who claim to follow Christ seemingly ignore His example of humility and service? Many are the plans in a man's heart, but it is the Lord's purpose that prevails. (See Proverbs 19:21.)

I once heard a song, "I Did It My Way." Sometimes doing it my way can include pushing and shoving others out of the way to get to a position that we feel belongs to us, or that we have convinced ourselves we deserve more. The road to success is littered with broken bodies left there by the more aggressive and viciously ambitious people. This type of betrayal runs rampant in our society. Brother will betray brother for a position that is coveted. Friend will "cut deep" another friend with betrayal on the way up to what is considered success, only to arrive there and find it is not all that and a bag of chips.

God has a plan for everyone, a destiny that He designed long before we were formed in the womb. Most of us, unfortunately, miss it because of selfish ambition and greed. This is why it is so clearly written in the Word of God that pride comes before the fall! (See Proverbs 16:18.) Then when it is too late, one sits back and wonders, "How did I get here? Why did I think it would be better than this? How was I so deceived?" Later when we see the people we let down or hurt we are left with regret and remorse.

REMORSE VERSUS REPENTANCE

Judas was supposed to be a friend to Jesus. They spent three years in ministry together; although Jesus knew that Judas would sell Him out, He loved him. I have often wondered if it was just the money that Judas was after when he betrayed Jesus, or if it was something else. Judas was in charge of the moneybag. It was the treasury that supported a ministry that consisted of thirteen men. There must have been a lot of money in it, even when Judas was stealing as much as he could.

Was thirty pieces of silver the only reason Judas betrayed Jesus? Could it have been that Judas felt that the Lord was not accomplishing the prophesy of freeing Israel in the manner that Judas thought He should? Was it that Jesus was no longer of use to him, so he betrayed him? After the betrayal, when Judas had the money in his hands, it stung his palms; it was blood money, the payment for his betrayal. Can't you just hear the coins hitting the floor and rolling all over the place as he threw the money back? There must have been a look of torment on his face and the feeling that his heart was ripping in his chest. He had betrayed his friend. Immediately after trying to return the money, and it was refused, Judas hung himself from a tree. So horrible was his death that the Bible tells us that his bowels gushed out.

You see, remorse is one thing, but repentance is another. Judas felt remorse for having betrayed Jesus, but he didn't repent. Instead of admitting his sin and turning from it, he chose to commit suicide. On the other hand, Peter swore, "I will lay down my life for you," on the same day that Peter denied he ever knew Jesus. (See Matthew 26:31–35, 69–75.) Although it is certain that Peter felt terrible remorse after having betrayed Jesus, he humbled himself, accepted his wrongdoing, and then repented. God restored him, and he was exalted to a position of leadership. Repentance is the way to go. Money, success, or advancement that is gained through betrayal never bears good fruit. The position may feel good for a while and the deceitful actions it took to attain it may seem justified. However, the Bible declares that "whatever a man sows, that he will also reap!" (Gal. 6:7).

Chapter 8
BETRAYED BY LOVE

IN THE YEARS that I have ministered, I have had the privilege of coming in contact with tens of thousands of teenagers. I have listened to their stories of betrayal by parents, friends, people at school, etc. These young adults deal with issues that leave gaping wounds that, if not tended to, can leave scars that affect their adult life.

Often we adults don't take seriously the emotional problems that affect our teens. For example, what we adults refer to as "puppy love" may be to a young person the most important relationship on the earth. Parents may brush aside a betrayal suffered by their children, thinking it's something that they will get over. Unfortunately, that is not always the case. Teen suicide is on the rise.* Some do it because they cannot deal with the wound of losing someone they loved and the feeling that they have been betrayed. Certainly this type of a tragedy doesn't occur every time a young couple breaks up, but the statistics are staggering nonetheless.

---

* Teen suicide is the 11th leading cause of death in the U.S. and the 8th leading cause of death for males. Suicide by firearms was the most common method for men and women, accounting for 55 percent of all suicides. For more information see www.familyfirstaid.org.

THE DEATH OF A BROKEN HEART

Jennifer held the cold metal gun in her palms. Looking down at it, she tried to blink back the tears that fell and wet the handle of the revolver. She threw back her head; the agony in her heart was tearing her apart. "How could Derrick do this to me? I loved him so much. I gave myself to him." Then a sob ripped out of her throat as feelings of anger, revenge, and bitterness filled her mind and heart.

She pressed the gun to her chest, weeping great tears. "This is the only way," she whispered. "My life is over; I can't go on without Derrick. I've been betrayed by the one I love." Her finger squeezed the trigger. Jennifer's body fell back on the bed. Her mom heard the shot and tapped on the door. "What was that noise, Jennifer?" she asked as she pushed the door open. Jennifer was slumped over on the bed, the gun still in her hand. "Jennifer, what have you done?" she screamed, lifting her daughter's lifeless body. Jennifer was pronounced dead from a bullet wound to her heart, a heart that had been broken by betrayal.

THE PROMISE

Jennifer was fifteen years old when she met Derrick at the school basketball game. He was sixteen years old and the cutest guy she had ever seen. After a victory game one night, they went out together for cokes with the gang. Sitting across from each other, Derrick was paying close attention to Jennifer. "I noticed you in math class a few weeks ago," he told her, striking up a conversation. "I wanted to ask you out, but I didn't think you'd want to go out with me. I heard that you were dating Dylan Lang, so I didn't want to interfere."

The mention of Dylan sent chills up Jennifer's spine. The breakup had been painful, and she was just getting over it.

Now here she was with this really cute guy Derrick, and she didn't want to think about Dylan anymore. Jennifer turned away for a moment as if to hide her embarrassment. "Dylan and I broke up about two weeks ago. Now he's dating Chloe, but I don't want to talk about that," she said. "Let's just talk about tonight. It was a great game. Aren't you glad we won?" Derrick smiled. "Yeah, I sure am." That night was the beginning of a long and very close relationship between Derrick and Jennifer. They were inseparable at school, at home, or on the phone. They just couldn't get enough of each other. Everyone at school referred to them as "the most popular couple." Jennifer was ecstatic. She loved Derrick and hoped to marry him someday.

The following year the relationship became even more serious. Derrick loved the lakeside, a place that he and Jennifer could go and spend time together. They had discovered a hiding place that looked like a cave. It sheltered them from the weather and they would spend hours there alone. One spring afternoon, they were strolling along the lake. "Let's go to our little hiding place, Jen," Derrick suggested. "I don't know," Jennifer protested. "We've been getting way too intimate lately, and we almost had sex the last time!"

"I know," Derrick said, apologizing, "but this time we'll be very careful, I promise. Trust me!" They crawled through the small opening of the rocks to the cave area. There was a towel left there from the last visit. Derrick spread it out and they sat down. Derrick began to tell Jennifer how much he loved her. "You're my everything, Jen," he cooed. "No one will ever take your place, no one!" Then they were in each other's arms. "Oh, Derrick," Jennifer said breathlessly, "Promise me you will always love me." Derrick kissed her passionately. "Always, Jennifer," he promised her. "I will love you always!"

Suddenly Jennifer sat up. Things were getting out of hand, "Derrick, don't. Please? I've never had sex with anyone before." Derrick pushed his hair back with his hands. It was obvious things were going too far, and it wasn't the first time that Jennifer had to call a halt. Then the debate they had every time they reached this point began: "Listen, Jen," Derrick started out, "you know that I love you and we intend to get married, don't we? Why, then, do we have to wait for something we will be doing anyway?" "But, Derrick," Jennifer argued, "I have never gone that far with anyone, not even Dylan. Please don't ask me," she begged. A look of frustration came over Derrick's face. "I'm not Dylan," he shot back sarcastically. "Let's go. It's obvious that I love you more than you love me."

Jennifer took his hand in hers and squeezed it gently, "That's not true. I love you as much, if not more." Derrick pulled her close. "Then prove it," he insisted. "Prove that you would go further with me than with Dylan and that I matter more!"

His lips were pressed hard against hers. Jennifer's emotions were in a tizzy. She wanted so much to make Derrick happy, and the thought of losing him to someone who would please him scared her. She pressed her body against his, her face reflecting a look of surrender. Derrick had won. She would prove she loved him. The experience was not a pleasant one. It was uncomfortable and it hurt. "But," she thought, "Now Derrick will always love me and never leave me. We are one!"

MOM'S CONCERN

Jennifer's mother began to worry. She expressed concern to her husband one Saturday morning after the kids had gone off to the lake. "Nothing to worry about, honey" he quipped. "They're good kids, and it's just a phase." But Mom couldn't shake the feeling, and she brought it up again after dinner.

"I don't know," she complained. "The kids are constantly together. Remember how attached Jennifer got to Dylan? We don't want a replay of that, do we?" Jennifer's father looked up from the dinner table, "Maybe you're not making too much of this honey. Let's plan a vacation this summer away from here and put some distance between the two of them."

As summer vacation approached, Jennifer was informed that they would be going to Martha's Vineyard for five weeks. "No, Mom," she complained. "I can't be away from Derrick. Can't we make other plans, please?" But the arrangements had been made. They were going!

After Jennifer was told, she ran over to Derrick's house and fell into his arms. "I can't believe it! They're separating us, and we won't be spending this summer together," she wailed. The two of them held each other close. "What are we gonna do, Jennifer?" Derrick asked in unbelief.

When school let out for the summer and it was time for Jennifer to leave, they tearfully said good-bye to one another. "I promise that I will call you everyday, Jen," Derrick promised. "I'll think about you and miss you terribly," she added. "I love only you," he told her. "Just you; no one else!"

Martha's Vineyard was beautiful. The flowers were all in bloom and the scent of them filled the summer air. The beach, with its white sand and blue surf, was inviting. As for Jennifer, she was sullen and refused to be comforted. She remained in her room looking out the window at all the activities going on outside. Mom had to literally drag her out, and getting her to eat was worse.

As for Derrick, he was crushed and refused to do anything until his love returned to him. His parents tried to coax him out by offering all kinds of entertainment, but it was futile. He wasn't budging. The young couple called each other every day complaining about how lonely they were and lost without each other.

ENTER CRYSTAL

One hot afternoon while Derrick was mowing the lawn, Crystal Cunnings, who lived across the street, came strolling over. For months she had been away at boarding school, but now she was home for summer vacation. Crystal was wearing a very sexy bathing suit. She had a great figure and knew how to show it off. It didn't take her long to notice how good-looking Derrick had gotten since she had seen him last. He had a dark tan and without his shirt his muscles looked great.

"Hey, Derrick," she called as she came up behind him, but he couldn't hear her over the roar of the lawnmower. Crystal tapped him on the shoulder to get his attention. Derrick whirled around and did a double take. Standing there was this beautiful girl that he hadn't seen in months.

"Hi, Crystal," he said, catching his breath. "Let me turn this thing off." He reached down and flipped the switch, killing the motor. He pulled a rag out of his back pocket and wiped the sweat off his face. Then he invited her to sit on the front porch. Crystal sat on the whicker chair and crossed her long, tanned legs. "Care for a cold drink?" Derrick offered. "No, thank you," she answered. "It's been quite a while since I saw you last," Derrick said. "You look great," he added, flashing a flirtatious smile. "You look pretty good yourself, Derrick," she flirted back. "Why don't we get together tonight and talk. Maybe you can fill me in on all the happenings since I've been away."

It was a tempting offer, but thoughts of Jennifer came racing in and Derrick decided to decline. "No, I'd better not. I'm dating Jennifer Thompson, and I don't think she would appreciate me hanging out with you." Crystal stood up to walk away, then paused, "Oh, come on Derrick," she insisted. "We've known each other since we were kids. A walk along the lake can't hurt, can it?" Derrick scratched his head, "OK, I'll meet you on the west dock at the lake tonight about nine."

It was a perfect night. The sky was filled with stars and the moon was full. There was a warm, balmy breeze coming off the water. Derrick arrived early and sat on the dock watching the last of the sailboats glide in. He missed Jennifer and wished she were there to share the beauty of the night with him. He had spoken to her but couldn't bring himself to mention that he would be spending the evening with Crystal.

The sight he saw before him shook him out of his thoughts of Jennifer. A short way up the beach he saw Crystal coming toward him. She was barefoot and wearing a long, white linen dress. Her honey-blonde hair was blowing in the light breeze as she walked along the shore. When she saw him she smiled and waved.

Derrick thought about how radiant she looked, and he wondered why he never noticed how beautiful she was before this. They passed the evening together talking about the neighborhood, the games they played as kids, and anything else that came up. "Wow, it's one o'clock in the morning," Derrick said as he glanced at his watch. "I'd better get back. I'm expecting a call from Jennifer."

THE BETRAYAL

When Derrick got home, there were several messages on the answering machine from Jennifer. She was frantic! He was hesitant to call her. What would he say? How would he explain that he had spent the evening with a gorgeous girl on the beach? When they talked that evening, Jennifer began to ask a lot of questions. "What do you mean you were with

Crystal?" she screamed in a jealous rage. "It was just an innocent evening," Derrick said defensively. Click! She slammed
the phone down in his ear.

After trying for two days to get her to answer the phone
without any success, Derrick decided to give it a break. "She'll
get over it and call me," he thought. Right about that time,
the phone rang. "Just as I thought," Derrick said aloud, "it's
Jennifer." To his surprise, the soft, sexy voice on the other end
of the line belonged to Crystal. "Hello, Derrick. So are you
up for another walk along the lake tonight?" Derrick swal-
lowed hard. "I really shouldn't," he answered. "Jennifer won't
even talk to me now." Crystal was determined and continued
to push: "Oh she's being silly. Let's just go for a short walk."
Derrick knew it wasn't a good idea, but he gave in. "OK," he
said. "You're right. She's being childish."

In the weeks that followed, Derrick saw a lot of Crystal.
They went to movies, had lunch, and spent long afternoons
sitting around her family pool and chatting. As time went on
and the two became closer, Jennifer's name came up less and
Derrick stopped calling Martha's Vineyard.

Then one afternoon while splashing around in the pool,
it happened. Derrick slipped his arms around Crystal's
waist, pulled her close, and kissed her. She responded by
wrapping her arms around his neck. What Derrick swore
would never happen, did. He was cheating on Jennifer and
was falling for Crystal. By the time summer ended, he and
Crystal also had sex.

When Jennifer arrived home, she went directly to Derrick's
house. She tapped on the door several times, but no one
answered. She was starting to panic. What was wrong? Why
hadn't he called her? Where was he? As these questions
were going through her mind, she made her way down the

driveway. Then she spotted Derrick sitting across the street with Crystal on her front porch. She was giggling, and he had his arm around her waist. When Derrick saw Jennifer coming toward him, he pulled his arm away and stood up. Crystal slipped away into the house and left the two of them alone. There was the look of guilt written all over his face. "Derrick, what's wrong? Why haven't I been able to get a hold of you? Where have you been? Why won't you talk to me?"

"Things are different now, Jen," he said, avoiding her eyes. "I've changed, and now I'm dating someone else. It happened while you were gone." Jennifer's knees began to shake. "Why are you doing this to me?" she cried, desperately. "Don't you know how much I love you? You are my whole world, Derrick," she shrieked in disbelief. "Please tell me you haven't started seeing Crystal. What about what we had together?" she screamed. "I gave myself to you!" There was a look of sadness in his eyes as he said, "Listen, Jen. I'm sorry, but it just happened. It wasn't planned." Having said that, he turned around and went into the house. Jennifer stood alone on Crystal's porch for a long time.

She told herself that the only way out of the pain of Derrick's betrayal would be to pay him back. Suicide was the answer. Jennifer went into her father's closet and pulled out his revolver. It was loaded. She walked into her bedroom and closed the door.

Derrick blamed himself for her death, even though it was not his fault. Jennifer's mom blamed herself, then she blamed Jennifer's father for not seeing the writing on the wall. However, the blame belonged to Jennifer alone. Her hasty decision resulted in a terrible tragedy.

Teen Suicide, Epidemic Proportions

This is a shocking story, but incidents like this one go on more then we would like to think or believe. As I said earlier, teen suicide is on the rise. In situations just like Jennifer's, teens respond in a variety of different ways. Some feel the betrayal is too great and cannot deal with having to go on without the one they cared for. Some isolate themselves for a time, trying to heal, while others enter into deep depression and cannot be consoled. Then there are those that go to the extreme and kill someone else or themselves in an act of revenge.

I knew a nineteen-year-old who was dating my youngest sister. One day he loaded a rifle, walked out into the morning air, and shot himself with her standing ten feet away. He died instantly. The night before, my sister had gone to the store during a party and while she was gone he had sex with one of the other girls. He was ridden with guilt, but rather than confess the mistake he had made, he convinced himself that suicide was the only way to remedy his betrayal.

There are countless groups in the music industry that sing songs about suicide and glorify it as the ultimate high, worthy of consideration. Every day our newspapers are filled with accounts of young people who have taken their lives due to depression, feeling abandoned, a family divorce, or change in relationships.

I have often counseled teenagers struggling with thoughts of suicide, and each time I remind them that suicide is not the end. Life is not ended when we die. Yes, it may be the end of life as we know it, but it cannot halt the inevitability of eternity. The problem does not go away; you just take it with you. Some tell me, "You don't know what I am going through!" My response? "You're going through, and you will get to the other side. There is an end to the hurt and the suffering. Why not work it out, get the help you need, and go on to live your life?"

Our young people need our attention and understanding. We must learn to listen and be sensitive to their feelings when they are trying to express their hurts and confusion. They deserve the same consideration that we require when we are hurting. Although their situation may seem insignificant to us, it may be very serious to them. In reality, the situation may be a small matter, but their feelings are not.

"I HATE DIVORCE," SAYS THE LORD.

There is another area in which our children suffer: divorce. While ministering recently, I called all the young people to the front of the church to pray for them each individually. As I walked down the line inquiring of their pain, the majority of them said they felt betrayed because either their mother or father had walked out on the family.

"How could my father do this to us, just abandon us? Doesn't he realize he is breaking our hearts?" one young girl cried, as I held her close to me. A young boy in big baggy shorts and an oversized Tommy Hilfiger T-shirt shook his arms in the air as large tears poured down his face. "I hate my father. How could he leave us? My mom feels so betrayed. He just walked out on us, Carol." When I prayed for him, he fell to the ground and lay there for a long time, wetting the carpet with his tears. Not far away stood three young girls, all about twelve years old, holding each other while they cried over the same hurt in their own lives.

Divorce not only affects the spouse, it takes other victims—the children. They don't understand. They feel responsible for the divorce, and they take it personally. They struggle with feelings of being abandoned, deserted, and ultimately thrown away, unwanted.

When I think of how our children and young adults have suffered in this generation, it brings tears to my eyes. I find problems like depression increasing. Despair attaches itself to them for various reasons, until finally many just give up on life. Drugs, alcohol, promiscuity and unwanted pregnancy, violence, street gangs, and prostitution in our society are at epidemic levels in countries all over the world. Our children must know their value and how desperately they are needed.

MAKING OR BREAKING BY THE WORDS WE SPEAK

Ministry must go beyond the adults. Churches must form outreaches to touch young adults that feel lost and broken. Having a pizza gathering on Friday night at youth group is not sufficient. As parents we need to concentrate on blessing our children and teenagers with the words of our mouth. Tell them that they are a blessing and a gift from God, encourage them in their endeavors, and speak words that are positive. Even during those times when they are doing the things that we hate and know are wrong, we should guard the words of our mouth. We certainly don't condone bad behavior, but calling them names, swearing at them, and telling them that they are no good will never make things better. Why not try calling those "things that are not, as though they were" (Rom. 4:17, NIV)?

We live in a negative world. Newspapers and the evening news all tell us the bad things that are going on in our world. Our homes should be a haven of rest from this atmosphere, a refuge of safety, and a place where the exalted Christ is worshiped. The family is a powerful, dynamic unit that

Satan is threatened by and seeks to destroy it. This is why the Scriptures admonish parents to "train up a child in the way he should go, And when he is old he will not depart from it" (Prov. 22:6). *Train* does not mean telling them what to do. It means doing it with them. The family unit has become fragmented, but when the Lord Jesus Christ is made the center of our family, we can come together on a daily basis and form a strong alliance with one another.

WATCH, LOOK, AND LISTEN

Betrayal in the family through divorce, abandonment, abuse, or just a lack of love is painful, and our children are suffering because of it. As adults we must protect our precious little ones. I know it's hard to find the balance between caring for teens and giving them the privacy they want and the respect they deserve. But if they are living in the house with you, you are responsible for them and it is your place to be aware of the decisions they are making both in and outside of the house.

Parents, I encourage you to reach out beyond yourself to receive one of the most precious gifts God will ever give you—your children. Listen to the sound of their voices. Try to detect if there is pain, confusion, depression, or even just the need for extra attention. Get involved with the things that your children enjoy and spend time doing those things together. Ask questions. Don't probe; just ask questions. If they open up and share what is in their heads and hearts, be open to listen. Sometimes just being silent and letting them unload does wonders.

Being caringly vigilant of one child, much less multiple children, can be very difficult for a single parent, especially if your spouse has abandoned you and you are now raising the children alone. If you are struggling, then I encourage you to inquire and search out one of the many organizations that have been formed to help families in crisis. Also, remember that if we will bathe our children in prayer and try to understand their problems, it can only make things better.

No Strings Attached

Young people, this part of my book is for you. I lived a rough life and more then once I thought about ending it by suicide—guns, pills, driving cars into walls. I struggled through life, never knowing where I was going and, as a result, going nowhere! I am so glad I never succeeded in taking my life. I got though it all and today I can look back and say, Thank God!

"This Jesus, is He for real?"

Listen, my precious friend, He's not a god that pops up on Sundays but leaves you alone throughout the week. He is a friend that truly cares about you. He isn't just some religious figure. Jesus is the embodiment of all that God is, and He is truly concerned for you and your life. Maybe sometimes you think nobody cares. I know; I thought that too. But someone does care, and the experience of knowing this wonderful friend can be yours by simply asking. You can do it now. It doesn't take a special place or any special prayer. Just as you are, you can ask Jesus to come into your life and He will! Simply say, "Jesus, please come into my heart. Forgive me for my sins, wash me clean, fill me with your Holy Spirit, and add my name to the Book of Life."

Let faith fill your heart and know that God sent Jesus for you. He loves you and has paid the price for all the things you have done wrong. He wants to make your life better; please believe that! Listen what the Lord says about you: "'For

I know the plans I have for you,' declares the Lord, 'plans to prosper you and not to harm you, plans to give you hope and a future'" (Jer. 29:11).

My precious friend, throughout life there will be many disappointments. We are wrapped in flesh, and it is likely at some point in your life someone will disappoint you. However, there is a friend you can count on. His name is Jesus, and when everyone you ever put your trust in and believed in walks out on you, He will always remain. That is a promise. When your heart is torn apart by things that are out of your control, He will love you and guide you with His eyes upon you. Call on Him today, and He will show you great and wonderful things! Say His name right now. Say it out loud: *Jesus*. It's the name that will set you free.

Chapter 9
BETRAYED BY GOD

I HAVE PRAYED FOR a tremendous amount of people whose hearts are bleeding as a result of having been betrayed. There have been times when some have cried in my arms and told me they feel like God has betrayed them. The following is the story of a man who felt that way.

Charlie was an all-around nice guy. He had a contagious laugh and a smile that would light up a room. Everybody loved him. If someone needed a helping hand, Charlie was the man for the job.

Charlie and his wife, Dawn, had three children. Jacob and Jordan, their twins, were seventeen years old. They both loved sports, had straight As at school, and were always honest, respectful, and helpful at home. Leah had just turned fourteen that fall. This sweet child was like a ray of sunshine, full of life and laughter. Leah got along wonderfully with the twins, always teasing and playing practical jokes on them. The boys were very protective and watchful when it came to their little sister, and she was Daddy's little angel to boot.

Charlie and Dawn had been married for twenty years. They were very happy together. Dawn had a good job as a teacher at the school, and Charlie was working for an engineering company for over twenty-five years. All was well, and the thought of anything interrupting this wonderful life was impossible, as far as Charlie was concerned.

DON'T PREACH TO ME!

Lou was Charlie's best friend. Saturday morning was their golf day. The two golfing buddies would meet on the course behind Lou' house to play nine holes. Two years back, Lou had been diagnosed with a fatal blood disease. He wasn't a religious person, but his wife went over to the local church. The prayer team began to pray for Lou, and in three months the blood disorder was gone. He was convinced that the prayers and his wife's faith in God brought on the healing. Having become a Christian, Lou wanted his friend Charlie to have the same wonderful experience, but Charlie wasn't interested.

One morning on the golf course, Lou started to tell Charlie about Jesus. "He'll give you a brand new life," he assured him. Charlie stopped before making his shot and turned to his pal. "Listen, Lou," he said, " I have a wonderful life. I have everything a man could ever want: a great wife, good kids, my health. What else could I possibly need?" He hit his shot; it landed on the green. "Anyway," he went on as he struck his club in his bag, "I don't do anything to hurt anyone. I try to be a nice guy."

Now it was Lou's turn. As he walked up to take his shot, he paused for a moment and leaned on his golf club. "Listen Charlie, it's not about being good. It's more than that. The Bible says, 'All have sinned and fall short of the glory of God.'" He turned and hit his shot. It landed in the bunker. Charlie let out a howl. "Good word, old man, but what a lousy shot."

THE MOST IMPORTANT DAY OF MY LIFE

One morning as Charlie sat at the breakfast table drinking his coffee and reading his morning paper, it started to rain. Dawn and the twins had already left, so it was just Charlie and Leah lagging behind, as usual. He glanced at the clock on the wall. It was seven thirty. He walked over to the stairway and shouted, "Leah, come on, angel. We are really running late this morning." Leah came bounding down the stairs. "Got any orange juice left, or did you scarf it all down, Daddy?" she asked jokingly. Her radiant smile revealed the braces on her teeth. Leah went over to the cupboard and reached in for a glass.

"You know what today is, don't you?" she asked her father. Charlie took the final gulp from his coffee cup. "No I don't. What is so important about today?" Leah walked over to the table, sat down, and poured herself a glass of orange juice. "It's only the most important day of my life," she said, surprised that he had forgotten. "Don't you remember, Daddy? It's the day I find out if I made the cheerleading squad!" Charlie laughed, "I'm sorry, honey. I didn't mean to forget the most important day of your life!"

Leah put her arms around Charlie's neck and squeezed lightly. "Oh, Daddy, you're always teasing me." She walked over to the counter and grabbed her purse and books. "Let me drive you over to Janna's," he offered. "No thanks, Daddy, I can run over, and besides, Janna's mom is driving us to school." Leah pushed open the screen door, stepped out, and looked over her shoulder. "I love you, Daddy," she said tenderly. Then she was gone. The screen door slammed shut behind her.

Charlie gathered up the dirty dishes off the kitchen table and started putting them into the dishwasher. That's when he heard it—a horrible sound as tires screeched, followed by a loud thump before it got quiet. He thought a dog had been hit. Through the screen door, he could see people rushing by. Charlie called out to one of the neighbors, "What's happened?" A voice rang out in response, "Someone call an ambulance! A girl has been hit by a car, and it looks pretty bad!" A cold chill ran through his body. "What girl?" he asked hoarsely.

DADDY, IT HURTS!

People from all over the block were gathering as Charlie approached the accident. He worked his way through the crowd. "Move back!" someone yelled. "Here comes her father." Charlie felt panic come over him. "Her father?" he thought. "What is going on?" The next thing he saw would haunt his dreams for many years to come. There she was laying on the street, his angel, his precious Leah. Her body was twisted in all different directions. Charlie knelt down beside her. His mouth was dry, perspiration was dripping from his forehead, and his hands were shaking. "Angel," he whispered, "talk to daddy." Charlie took her limp hand in his. It was cold and wet from the rain. Leah's eyes fluttered. For a moment. she focused on his face. "Daddy," she whispered, "please help me. It hurts so bad," then she slipped into unconsciousness.

The shrill of the siren on the ambulance filled the air. It pulled up; two men in uniforms jumped out and began to push back the crowd. The men began to examine the injured girl. "Please, mister," they urged Charlie, "let us do our job. It looks serious. Please move aside." Charlie was numb; he couldn't speak, but he moved aside. They frantically rushed about, talking on the radio to the hospital where Leah would be transported. A neck brace was placed gently around her neck, and an IV drip was attached to her arm. Within ten minutes she was lifted on a gurney into the back of the ambulance. "Charlie, can I be of any assistance? Can I contact anyone?" Charlie turned to where the voice was coming from. It was his next-door neighbor, Ed. "Yes, please," Charlie responded. "Call the school and have my wife come to the hospital immediately."

The ambulance driver called out, motioning for Charlie to climb into the back of the ambulance. "Sir, you can ride with us," he said. Charlie climbed in and sat down next to where Leah was laying. He could hear soft moans coming out of her throat. She looked helpless and so very pale. Charlie started mumbling, "She was fine…She ran out the door. I was going to drive her to her friends. I don't understand what happened…" his voice trailed off.

He was trembling violently. "Just relax, sir," the attendant told him. "We will be at the hospital in just a few minutes." The ambulance door shut behind them and the vehicle sped off. It was needling its way through traffic, the siren screaming. "Is she going to be alright?" he asked the attendant. "I'm sorry, sir. I'm in no position to answer that. It appears she has broken bones and her head is swollen."

When they arrived at the hospital, Leah was rushed into the emergency room. A team of doctors including their private physician was waiting. Dr. Henley put his hand on Charlie's shoulder. "Just go in the waiting room, Charlie," he said gently. "I will keep you posted. We are doing everything possible to save Leah." Charlie did as the doctor ordered and went into the waiting room. He had been sitting there about ten minutes when Dawn burst through the door. Her face was contorted with fear and confusion. "Charlie, my goodness! What has happened?" He pulled her against him, choking on his words he told her, "It's Leah. She was hit by a car. It's bad honey. It's real bad!"

STILL IN THE WOODS

The rest was a maze. Leah was rushed into the operating room and after that into the CCU unit. When Dr. Henley came out, he looked exhausted. He took Charlie and Dawn into a private room where they could discuss Leah's condition. Dr. Henley had known the family for years, but this was the first time he had to face them with this sort of tragedy. He took his glasses off and rubbed his eyes, before looking up at his friends. "Charlie, I've known you and Dawn for twenty years. I delivered all three of your children, so I am going to shoot strait with you. Leah was hit very hard, and it has broken several bones. Both her legs are broken—the femur in the left leg, and the tibia and fibula in the right leg. She has three broken ribs, and her lung was punctured. The liver is damaged, and we removed her spleen. Besides that, her head is badly swollen and her heart is very weak." He paused for a moment, took a breath, and continued. "It was a long operation, all touch and go, and right now she is unconscious," he concluded.

Dawn put her hands to her face and began sobbing, "Oh, my baby! What has happened to my baby?" Her husband reached over to comfort her, but she pulled away. "Where were you, Charlie? Why weren't you watching her," she wailed. Charlie's face was white as the hospital walls. "Tell me the truth, doctor. Will she be all right?" The doctor stood up, "I think I should prepare you for the worst. If she makes it through the night she will have a better chance, but I repeat, she is critical. Medically we have done all we can.

When Lou got the news, he and his wife rushed to the hospital to be with Charlie and Dawn. "Our church is praying for Leah and your family, as well," he told them.

Finally after what seemed like an eternity, Charlie and Dawn were escorted to Leah's bedside in the critical care unit. When they got there, Dawn almost passed out. The scene was horrendous. There were tubes in Leah's nose, throat, and arms. The machines she was hooked up to were beeping everywhere. Dawn turned to her husband. "Look at her; she doesn't even look like herself," she cried out. Her face and head are all swollen and it looks like she's not breathing!" The nurse came rushing over and cautioned, "Please try not to raise your voice. I know she doesn't look like herself, but that's the swelling." She ushered Dawn to a chair. "Sit here. I will get you a glass of water." Dawn sat there staring at her precious daughter. Just hours ago, everything was just fine. Now she was fighting for her life. This whole thing was a horrible nightmare.

Charlie walked out into the waiting room. His friend Lou was there with the twin boys. They were holding up okay, but they wanted to go in and see their sister. The CCU allowed only one visitor at a time, so they had to wait their turn. When they saw the helpless condition their little sister was in, they cried. Time marched on. The doctor came in; the doctor went out. Leah's condition remained critical.

Then late one afternoon at about five o'clock, Leah woke up. Her lips were swollen and cracked, and she could barely open her eyes. Tears trickled down the sides of her face. "Welcome back, darling," her father said as he gently stroked her arm. "You've been out a long time. Daddy's here, and Mom will be here shortly."

Dr. Henley came in. "Leah woke up, Doc. That's a good sign, right?" Charlie asked optimistically. The doctor looked down at the chart. "I don't want to give you any false hope, Charlie. Leah's still in critical condition, and her heart is still very weak."

Every three hours, the nurse would come in with morphine to help with the pain. Leah had casts on both her legs. Her head was wrapped in a big bandage, and her ribs were wrapped as well. Only after a shot did she feel any relief, and as soon as it wore off, the pain would return. Leah was suffering terribly, and hope was grim.

DADDY, I WANT JESUS IN MY LIFE

Days after Leah had awakened from the coma, Charlie was snoozing on the chair next to the bed. "Daddy?" she barely whispered through parched lips. He sat up abruptly, "Hey, angel, you're awake. Should I get the nurse to get you a pain shot?" Leah shook her head, "No, I need to ask you a favor." "Don't strain yourself, honey," Charlie cautioned. "You need all of your strength to get well." Leah looked around the room and then focused on her father's face. "Daddy," she said softly, then paused to work up the strength to go on, "I want to talk to Lou, please." "What is it you want, angel," her father asked, but she was too weak to finish.

Suddenly, the nurse rushed over with her pain shot. Leah moved her head, "No, wait please. Daddy, I want to ask Jesus into my heart," she said breathlessly. Charlie's expression became serious, "Okay honey, I'll have Lou here tomorrow." Leah forced out the words, "No, Daddy, right away." The nurse insisted that she take the pain shot, and the needle was inserted into her hip. A moment later she slipped into a deep sleep.

That night, Lou came to her bedside. Leah woke up and smiled weakly when she saw him there. With tears streaming down his face, Lou led Leah to the Lord. After they prayed, he read the gospel of John to her. That was the first night Leah slept peacefully without pain medication.

The next day, the twins came in to see their sister. "It's time for us all to be saved," Leah whispered. "I know, Leah," Jordan said. "Jacob and I have been thinking about it a lot lately." At that moment, Charlie walked over to the bed and stood next to his sons. They bowed their heads and the three of them asked Jesus Christ to come into their hearts, just as Leah had done the night before. The next day, Lou presented Charlie with his first Bible. He sat at Leah's bedside and read, "For God so loved the world that He gave His only begotten Son, that whoever believes in Him should not perish but have everlasting life."

One evening, Leah had been awake for a longer period of time than normal. She looked over to where her mom and dad were sitting. She began to talk, her most determined voice still little more than a breathless whisper. Suddenly, words began to flow over Leah's lips: "I know I am going to be with Jesus," she told them. "I know I am going there." Charlie took his daughter's hand. "You are not going anywhere sweetheart," he told her gently. "Don't talk like that. God is going to heal you, I know it." She moved her head from side to side, and a smile came over her face. "No, Daddy, don't be afraid for me. I'll be okay."

The next morning, Charlie was sitting beside his daughter praying. He felt a slight touch. When he looked up, Leah was smiling at him. Her voice was clear, "Daddy I love you and mom and the boys, and I know because of Jesus we will spend eternity together. But I know I have to go on ahead." Charlie stopped his daughter, "No, angel, you are going to get better. Just rest." Then the most incredible thing happened. Leah looked over at the window. "Look, Daddy," she said, "aren't they beautiful?" Her father looked toward the window. He didn't see anything. Then he heard Leah draw a deep breath, and when she expelled it, she was gone. His precious angel Leah had peacefully slipped away.

WE'LL ALL BE TOGETHER AGAIN SOMEDAY

At the funeral, Charlie stood at the casket looking down at his precious child. She looked so beautiful and peaceful. He wouldn't move. He stood there all day, staring and weeping.

When it came time to close the casket, Charlie protested, "No, don't put her in the dark. Don't put my baby in the ground." Lou walked over in an attempt to calm him down, but Charlie was inconsolable.

Several weeks after Leah was buried, Lou walked over to Charlie's house. "My friend," Lou started out, "please let me pray and comfort you." Charlie flew into a rage. "Get away from me and take your God with you! He betrayed me! I believed in Him and He took my little angel!"

One afternoon a few weeks after Leah had passed away, Charlie was sitting in the living room in front of the television, staring. His son Jacob walked into the room, came up to his father, and knelt down in front of him. "Dad, can we talk?" he asked. "There is something I have to say to you." Charlie looked at his son. "Sure, Jacob. What is it?" "Dad, I miss Leah terribly, and so does Jordan. I know mom is having a hard time as well." Then he placed his hand on his father's knee and said sadly, "But Dad, now we are beginning to miss you too."

At that moment, Jacob's twin brother Jordan walked through the front door. He came into the living room and asked what was going on. "I was just telling Dad that I don't believe that God has betrayed us." Jacob told him, "He knows what its like for His child to die because He sent Jesus to die for us." Tears filled Jordan's eyes. "I feel the same way,

Dad," he added. "I don't understand why Leah had to die. The thing is that it's not for us to ask why Leah died, but why she was born. Dad, she brought us so much joy, but above all she led us to the Lord."

When he finished the three of them broke into tears. Charlie cried for a long time, holding his sons close to him. Then he stopped and wiped his eyes. He looked at his two sons; it had been a long time since he had paid any attention to them. Then he said, "I don't know if I will ever get over losing your sister; sometimes I feel like the grief is more than I can bear. But you are right. She showed us something that death couldn't steal—the truth about Jesus—and one day we will be reunited with her because of Him! This is the blessed hope, our salvation."

That night in prayer, Charlie repented for blaming God for the death of Leah. From that day forward things began to change in Charlie's family. Today he and his wife Dawn work with victims of tragedy, offering them the same hope they received in the midst of their trial.

Some Things Remain a Mystery

There are people that have lost loved ones who go through life blaming God, as did Charlie. They feel betrayed by Him. They ask questions like: Did He ignore my prayers? Was I unworthy? Why do the good die young, while others that go about hurting people and doing wrong live long and sometimes very healthy lives; it just doesn't seem fair!

There are many stories of people who shake their fists toward heaven and blame God for tragedy in their lives. I know a woman, Diana, who I consider to be as pure as the driven snow. Diana is faithful to God, her husband, her family and all that know her. She is considered a virtuous woman.

One afternoon, while driving her nephew to a park, she pulled out onto a country road and was hit by a large truck. Both she and her nephew were nearly killed.

After Diana's recovery, her mom began to ask a series of questions about God. "How could this happen to you?" she asked her daughter. "You never do anything to hurt anyone. I don't understand God." It was during one of these conversations that Diana stopped her mother in mid sentence and said, "Listen, Mom, it's not God's fault. I still believe in God and trust Him as much as I ever did. The fact is I didn't see the truck. That's it, Mom; I just didn't see the truck coming and I pulled out."

We don't have all the answers. No one does. I have resigned myself to accept the fact that there are many things in life I don't understand. I do believe, however, that God is not killing or hurting people. The devil is loose, and he is the author of death and sickness. I have asked many questions through the years, and some God has graciously answered, while others remain a mystery. However, of this I am sure: there will come a day when we will understand everything. The Word promises that, "For now we in a mirror, dimly, but then face to face. Now I know in part, but then I shall know just as I am also known" (1 Cor. 13:12). In the meantime, I will continue to trust the Lord with all my heart and lean not on my own understanding. I will acknowledge the Lord in all my ways, and He will make my path straight! (See Proverbs 3:5–6.)

Chapter 10
BETRAYED BY PARENTS

W HY IS IT that we are so lenient with our own weaknesses and sins, yet so quick to judge others and hold their sins against them? There was a time I was guilty of this. I held bitterness in my heart for years toward someone whom I felt had betrayed me: my mother.

I was one of ten children—the fourth from the oldest, and six siblings followed me. Each one of us was one or two years apart in age. My mother was like a gerbil, constantly giving birth.

DIFFERENT THAN THE REST

I was told that when I was born, unlike the others, I had a growth of red fuzz that started on my head and grew down my back. Mom said I looked like a little monkey. This description was not meant to insult, but to me it was obvious that from the very beginning I looked different from the rest of her children. I grew up feeling like I was the least favorite. (I was convinced that every parent of multiple children has one child that stands out as his or her favorite, and my mother was no exception.) I don't remember my mother ever telling me that she loved me—not once—nor can I remember a tender moment, a hug, or other kind word. I lived much of my young life with the terrible feeling that I was probably unplanned and unwanted.

In the early years of marriage when my mother was pregnant every other year, she became aware of the fact that my father had been unfaithful to her on more then one occasion. This revelation spurred in her a rage that gave birth to a violent streak. Our house became more of a battlefield than a home, and the weekends were the worst. They would go on an "all day long" drinking spree together. After an entire day at the local bar, they would return home. What went on before they walked in the door of the house was never clear, but extremely violent fights always broke out. Furniture was turned over and dishes thrown out of the cupboards. Sometimes the windows were smashed. There were splats of blood on the walls, my mom's clothes ripped and my father's face scratched.

All of this took place while the children were screaming and the police were pounding at the door warning my parents that they were disturbing the peace. It was a fiasco! With the combination of alcohol, violence, and infidelity, we were as dysfunctional as you can get. I was convinced that if you looked up *dysfunctional* in the dictionary you would find a picture of our family!

You're Stupid

It was Father's Day, and I was about eight years old. I decided that I could win my dad's love by making a special handmade present. I took four popsicle sticks and some plastic wrap and made a frame. I found a piece of paper and drew flowers on it. Then I added a very special poem, written right from my heart. I stuck it on some cardboard and placed it in the frame. When I looked at my special gift, I was sure my dad would be proud of me. After all, I had made it with my own hands.

I found him in his room standing in front of the window, piddling around in his drawer. I approached. "Daddy," I said cautiously, "this is for you. Happy Fathers Day!" My little arms reached forward and handed him the little frame. To my knowledge, none of the other kids had done anything for him on this day. He took it out of my hand as I stood there waiting patiently with my little heart pounding. When he had finished reading it and examining it, he turned to me and said something that absolutely broke my heart: "You're stupid, and this is stupid!" At that, he handed my little gift back to me. It was junk and he didn't want it.

I stood there stunned, held in the grip of rejection. He went right back to what he was doing, as if I had never approached him. I walked away, my heart crushed in my chest. I went outside to the garage and opened the lid of the garbage can. Taking one last look at the poem that I had written especially for my daddy, I tossed it into the can and watched it fall to the bottom, breaking into pieces. From that day forward, I was determined never to seek his affections again.

WHOSE CHILD AM I?

When I was in my teens, my father was confined to a mental institution. Several times he escaped and came home, but the police would come and return him to the mental hospital. All week my mother went to work trying to make a decent living for her kids, and on weekends she would drive eighty miles back and forth to the hospital to visit her sick husband. The loneliness eventually led her to the arms of other men. It was during this time that she introduced me to someone who she thought might be my real father.

I was home in bed when the phone rang. It was my mother. She was at a bar about two miles up the road. "Come and pick me up" she said. "I have someone I want you to meet." I looked at the clock beside the bed and saw that it was three o'clock in the morning. I didn't have a license, but the thought of having the opportunity to drive the car woke me up quick. I walked through the house past my little sisters and brothers, who were all snuggled in their beds. A few minutes up the street wouldn't matter, I thought. I pulled on my shorts and T-shirt, grabbed the keys to the car, and out the door I went.

I drove slowly down the deserted streets to the bar. When I pulled up, I noticed that there was only one other car in the parking lot. I walked in and saw my mother standing in a dark corner. I could tell she had a lot to drink. Beside her stood a handsome man in his forties. He was tall with dark, curly hair and striking features. I approached cautiously and curiously.

He looked down at me with an affectionate stare. My mother said, "Pat, this is Carol." I just stood there. I didn't know who he was. I just assumed Mom was drunk and wanted to introduce me to her friend. I felt a fluttering in my stomach as our eyes met. It was as if I had known this man, yet to my knowledge I had never seen him before this night. He placed his hand on my shoulder. "Would you like to give Pat a hug, Carol?" my mother asked. I put my arms around his neck, then quickly pulled away and went over to sit down at one of the empty tables.

After a few minutes, the bartender announced that it was closing time and the lights were being turned off. There was a clinking of glasses as the bartender washed the last of them and put them on the shelf. Pat walked my mother and I to the car. He paused and looked over at me. "I've waited a long time to meet you, Carol," he said softly. I smiled shyly and added, "Nice to have met you, too." He got in his car and drove off. I never saw him again after that night.

I helped my mother into the car and got in on the driver's side. It started to sprinkle, so I reached over her and closed the window on her side. I then pulled the car out of the parking lot and started to make my way down the road toward home. It was now four thirty in the morning. The smell of alcohol filled the car. As I drove along, I thought about the man, Pat, that I had been introduced to. "Mom, who was that man?" I asked. My mother took a deep breath, and in a slow, alcohol-induced tone she whispered, "When I was twenty-four years old, I made a mistake, and I had an affair with him. I think he is your father."

I Won't Get Mad; I'll Get Even

My entire body froze. My thoughts went crazy, and I felt like I had been hit with a ton of bricks. What was she saying? I knew this wasn't just a drunken statement. There was something about that man. Didn't my heart burn in me when he said hello? Didn't his eyes seem to look right through me? I was stunned. I looked over at her with my mouth hanging open. I started to ask her what all this meant, but it was too late; she had passed out cold.

That night I crawled into my bed and lay there wide awake staring at the ceiling with a thousand thoughts running through my head. Hot tears flowed down my face, staining my pillow. The next day my mother had no recollection of the night before. The subject did not come up until fifteen years later, but I carried that night in my heart and went over it in my mind a millions times.

I learned to hate the man I had called father, and resented my mother just as much. It became increasingly obvious that I was a thorn in her side. I deliberately became pregnant out of wedlock and flaunted it to punish her. In the years I was addicted to drugs, I would come to the house stoned out of my mind to taunt and aggravate my mother. When my father died alone in a motel room in North Carolina having escaped the mental hospital, I was relieved. I lived in bitterness and brokenness with a nagging feeling of being disconnected from the family I was sure I was not a part of. The pain of thinking that I was an illegitimate child never left me.

When I was diagnosed with chronic active hepatitis B and given a short time to live, I never contacted my family. I was a helpless and hopeless drug addict, deeply involved in witchcraft and New Age philosophy. Full of hate and vengeance, I was unabashedly out of control. Any encounter with my mother would end in us arguing. It seemed clear to me that she was happier when I wasn't around, so I stayed gone as much as possible. At holidays I seldom visited or called. If I showed up at all, I was full of drugs and ready to make a scene.

Chapter 11
THE DIVINE APPOINTMENT

IN JUNE OF 1980, I attended a Friday night service at the Full Gospel Tabernacle. Pastor Tommy Reid had invited a young evangelist who had a healing ministry to come and preach. His name was Benny Hinn. When I entered the church that night, it was packed to capacity. I was dressed in tight jeans and a blouse opened down the front. My hair hadn't been washed for days and there were black circles under my eyes from weeks of shooting drugs. I was as high as a kite. Linda, the young woman who had invited me to come, spotted me when I walked in. I wasn't hard to miss. Linda was visibly surprised to see me, but she had saved a seat for me in hope and there I was! Just as we were seated the service began.

JESUS, HEAL HER

In my head I could hear various voices, some telling me to run out of the church, others that just tormented me. I knew it was the spirits that I had invited into my life through my involvement in witchcraft and New Age philosophy. Through the years, I was constantly plagued with mental problems that developed into a violent nature. In my daily use of drugs, I would deliberately take too much, hoping they would take my life. I was in an abusive and unhappy marriage, filled with infidelity and drugs. I figured I didn't have anything to live for, and on top of it I was walking around with a death sentence hanging over my head as a result of my illness. I had accepted the invitation to church not because I was looking for any real hope, but rather was trying to appease a nice Christian girl who had been very kind to me.

However, God had big plans for me that night, and my life was about to go in a very different direction. The preacher on the platform was talking about a man named Jesus. He told the crowd that this great man was the Son of God, who loved people and wanted to change their lives and heal their bodies. I sat there in a terrible, tormented state, as the demons that had ruled my life up to that time did not want to give me up to the other side. But the power of God was so strong that night that no demon in hell could withstand it. I decided to take that long walk to the altar to meet this Jesus if He would have me. I got up, my legs feeling like they were sinking in sand. I kept walking until I reached the platform. When the evangelist saw me, he was awestruck. "Bring that young woman up here," he ordered the ushers. I was taken to he where he was standing.

The man looked at me with pity in his eyes. It was obvious that I was lost and tormented by demons and drug addiction. He began to pray and instructed the congregation to do the same. I was totally confused at the thought of strangers praying for me in what seemed to be a holy setting, but I watched as small children went to prayer and teenagers raised their hands as they asked God to save my soul. Grown men were crying, all for me—a demon-possessed, drug-addicted, dying witch.

Suddenly, I heard the evangelist cry out in a loud voice, "Dear Jesus, precious Jesus, heal her!" What happened next is nothing less then phenomenal. As the church prayed, the power of God hit that place like an earthquake. I felt this electrical serge travel from my head to my toes. I fell to the ground like a board and lay there. From the floor I heard Benny's voice like thunder overhead. "Don't touch her," he cried out. "God is doing something here!" While I lay on the floor of that church, I had a fascinating experience with Jesus Christ. He made Himself known to me and His love filled me in the most wonderful way. I was absolutely amazed at the love of God's Son and the experience I was having with Him.

A BRAND NEW LIFE

I was healed of chronic hepatitis B, as well as bleeding ulcers. I was delivered from the addiction to drugs, and my mind was healed of mental illness. For the first time, I felt the love of God fill my life and begin to clean out spirits and the rest of the terrible things I had given myself to. I was totally changed into another person—saved, delivered, and set free. As I was making my way off the platform, feeling an incredible surge of love flowing through me, I heard a voice say, "Young lady." It was the evangelist. I looked at him and he said with a booming voice, "You will never be the same. Never." And he was right. I would never be the same.

Now I was on a new road, one of life, not death. I was a new creature, living and loving life. I wasn't going to die. I was feeding my mind with the Word of God on a daily basis and attending The Full Gospel Tabernacle Church. I made it a point to be there every time the doors were opened. I couldn't get enough of the wonderful teachings of Pastor Tommy Reid.

It was an exiting life, full of joy unspeakable. It was great to be alive, and I wanted to serve God and His people with all my heart. Suddenly, things in my life went full speed ahead. I received a call to preach the gospel, and God opened doors immediately. Before long, I went on the road spreading the good news. It was awesome!

Chapter 12
FORGIVE ME, GOD, BUT NOT HER!

M Y SISTER KATHY was always the religious one of the family. But although she had knowledge of God, she had never been born again. I told her about my experience with the power of God and my conversion. Kathy was intrigued and wanted to know the Lord as I had come to know Him. We prayed together and she was beautifully saved. We were so happy and spent hours in the Word of God and prayer together.

A CONSCIENCE NAMED KATHY

About eight months later, Kathy called me. She was very excited. "Carol," she said in a bubbly voice, "Mom has accepted the Lord. Isn't that wonderful?" Internally, I was totally unmoved, but I lied and acted like I was as happy too. In my heart of hearts, I was still toting around that rock of bitterness and unforgiveness. "It's fine that she is saved," I told myself, "as long as I don't have to hear her or see her." My mother was living in Arizona and I lived in Florida, so we were miles apart. That suited me just fine!

Then it happened. Kathy and I had to go to Arizona for a family emergency. Kathy had arranged it so that we would be staying at our mother's apartment. As the old expression goes, I was as nervous as a long-tailed cat in a room full of rocking chairs. This would be my first encounter with my mother since her conversion.

After the plane had ascended into the clouds, Kathy began telling me things that I really wasn't ready to hear. "God is dealing with you, Carol," she began. I looked at her as I munched on my scrawny little bag of peanuts. "Just exactly what are you talking about?" I asked with disgust in my voice. "Oh, just the fact that you are preaching the gospel and telling people they have to love and forgive one another, and you haven't forgiven mom," was her rather blunt reply. I was appalled. "That's not true," I argued. "Oh, but it is, Carol, and you must deal with this unforgiveness in your heart toward mom once and for all. This is the reason that God has you going to Arizona!"

I was instantly aggravated and wanted Kathy moved to another seat, or, better yet, moved out on the wing for the duration of the flight. Unfortunately, the plane was full and she wasn't going anywhere. It appeared that her divine assignment for this trip was to be my conscience. "Oh brother," I moaned.

The flight down into Phoenix was a bit bumpy. I looked out the tiny window at the ground below to see mountains stretching across the land, blanketed in fog. Three bells sounded to announce that we were cleared for landing. The air was stifling hot when we got off the plane. It was August in Arizona, and the temperature was a hundred and ten degrees. I was baking. My mom and my brother's wife, Jacque, met us at the airport. I gave Jacque a warm hug, but I pulled away quickly when it came time to hug my mother. I couldn't look into her eyes. She had no problem looking into mine, and it was clear she was very glad to see me. The change in her as a result of her conversion was instantly noticeable, yet I could not bring myself to feel endearing or loving toward her.

DOES IT SHOW?

The ride from the airport was relatively short. When we got to mom's apartment, I disappeared into the bathroom as soon as I could. I looked into the mirror and asked myself, "Did it show? Did my feelings toward Mom show?" I wiped the sweat off my brow and refreshed my lipstick before I ventured out into the kitchen where the girls were chattering excitedly. I could smell the scent of freshly brewed coffee. I poured myself a cup and joined the others at the table.

My mother couldn't say enough about her conversion. She told us that she no longer drank alcohol on a daily basis. Her experience with Jesus had transformed her, and she was truly in love with Him. As for me, I wasn't having it. I sat there with a fake smile and sipped my coffee. Then I excused myself. "I am really tired from the trip," I lied. My mom was disappointed that I was retiring so early. "Okay, honey." she said with a smile. "You have a good sleep. I'll see you in the morning."

I crawled on the top bunk to allow "my conscience" to sleep on the bottom. She came in a few minutes later and I could hear her praying. Then I heard her whisper, "Pssst, Carol, You awake?" I turned over abruptly; "I am now, Kathy!" Suddenly her head was peeking over the edge where I was laying. "Carol, this is your opportunity to make things right with Mom." Now I was fuming. "Knock it off, Kathy. I'm fine with Mom. I love her," I said with tight lips. Kathy's response was quick: "No! You don't. You are hurt, and you must talk this thing out. At least consider it, Carol. Please?"

"Anything to appease her," I thought as I replied, "Okay I will. Now let me go to sleep!"

I lay there in the darkness with thoughts of the past filling my head. A rock the size of a small meteor filled my heart. "I'm trying to love her," I said to God in the dark, "really I am. It's just…" My prayer trailed off and I fell into a deep sleep, but not before a tear slipped down my cheek.

THE SETUP

After we had completed the business-related components of our trip, Kathy was relieved because she was ready to get down to the real reason God had brought us to Arizona and to my mother's house.

That evening after dinner, Debbie, my younger sister, with whom I had been very close when we were children, came over to my mom's apartment. She lived a few buildings away in the same complex. I was overjoyed to see her and found myself clinging to her to get some relief from my ever-present companion and conscience, Kathy.

The four of us sat around sipping Cokes, talking, and passing the time. It was kind of nice and I began to relax, though I was still diligently observing my mother as she testified of her love for the Lord and her new life. Then Debbie stood up and stretched as she said, "Listen girls, I'm tired. I gotta go. Let's all meet at the pool in the morning and get some relief from this heat." I felt panic come over me as the door closed behind her. "Oh no," I thought, "I'm left with my mother and my conscience."

Kathy, saw her window of opportunity. She stood up and began heading down the hall to the bathroom, cooing, "I'm going to take a shower, then I'm going to bed. You two just sit there and talk." All I could think about for the next few minutes was how I was going to drown Kathy in the pool the next day.

Now sitting alone with Mom, I decided that I was going to finally face this thing and confront her. I started from the beginning, pointing out all the times I felt unloved and pushed aside. I complained about the lack of love and affection in our relationship. I pointed out the mistakes she made in the way she brought me up. I shot questions at her at rapid speed, but would point out more of her failings before she could answer. "And how about the time you told me that I was somebody else's kid?" I bellowed. "That tormented me for years. Why was I treated like that? I felt so betrayed by you."

My mother sat there in silence, expressionless, as I continued to blast her with her past. She just listened intently. Not once did she try to defend herself or argue her side of the story. Finally I simmered down and looked across the room at her. How would she answer? I knew that I was right. "She had it coming," I thought, defensively. "You never told me you loved me, Mom," I said sadly, "and you never held me, ever! If you only had enough love for just a few, why did you have so many kids?"

A Simple Answer

I was finished. I sat there quiet, waiting for an answer—*the* answer that would heal the years of torment and hurt that I felt she was responsible for. My mother sat up in her chair. She looked at me and shook her head before beginning, "You know, Carol, I haven't a hint why I couldn't express love. Maybe I just never knew how." Her face had a soft expression. Her beautiful brown eyes looked childlike and her voice was apologetic. She paused for a moment. I could see she was searching for answers, answers she didn't have. "No one knows more than me the wrong I've done. I am painfully aware of the hurt I have caused and the mistakes I have made."

She then looked over at me with sadness in her eyes. "And as for the man I told you was your father, he's not. All of you children have the same father, of that I am absolutely certain! I was young when I met Pat. Your father had been unfaithful to me, and I was looking to be noticed and loved. So I fell into an affair with a married man. I was so young. When I became pregnant, I wanted to believe that you were his child, but I knew that it wasn't true." A sad look came over her face as she finished. "What I told you was wrong. I am sorry that it hurt you so deeply and for so long, but I can't change that now." A lump the size of the Rock of Gibraltar formed in my throat. "I'm a different person now, Carol," she said tenderly. "I'm forgiven for my sins, just as you were for your sins." When she finished there was absolute silence. There wasn't anything left to say.

I'm a Hypocrite

Then it dawned on me. Hadn't I gone to God with all my failures, and didn't He graciously forgive me and remember my sin no more? The Lord brought such light and wisdom to me that night. He showed me how I had walked into my new life with Him carrying excess baggage, including resentment. There I was, sitting before my mother like some sort of a judge, condemning her for all her past mistakes and accusing her of betraying me. I dumped on her for the rejection and resentment that I felt. "She was to blame; she was the cause," I thought as I justified the years of bitterness I felt toward her.

The Lord had forgiven her as He had forgiven me, yet I had held my mother's sins against her. I was forgiven, but she didn't deserve to be, was that it? I began to see how wrong I had been. Suddenly I was hit with the stark reality of life: we all make mistakes, and we all mess up. My mother was a young woman trying to make her way through life, and along the way she made a lot of mistakes just like everyone else, including me. God forgave me and commanded me to forgive others as I had been forgiven, but I had refused to do that. I was learning a hard truth. Though it wasn't easy to accept, I knew I had no choice because of God's command to love.

We go to God everyday with our sins. We pray, "Forgive me, Lord," and He does instantly, without any question. The Lord is full of mercy and grace, yet when others sin against us we refuse to forgive. We are sure that the people who hurt us should suffer. We convince ourselves they don't deserve our forgiveness because their mistakes caused us so much pain. Yes, my mother's mistakes affected my life, but she never told me to go out and make the same mistakes she made. I made those decisions myself.

That evening when I said good-night I walked over to my mother, the woman who had carried me in her womb and given birth to me, and I embraced her. When I decided to forgive as I was forgiven, it was the greatest release of my life. For the first time in my life, as I held my mother I felt the love and affection she had for me. My mother was able to give me the love I needed because she had experienced it herself though the Lord. Today it is obvious to all of her children that she loves us equally. I can only wonder how much I would have missed had God not sent me to Arizona with Kathy!

FREE THE PRISONER

Don't be locked in a self-made prison of unforgiveness. We can choose to forgive or keep the hate. There are times when the betrayal is too painful and we can't seem to get past the hurt to forgive the person, but that is when we have to allow the Holy Spirit to go into the depths of our hearts and let His healing power set us free. This has to be an act of our own will, God will not force us. He will make a way and make it possible for us to forgive by first "shedding His love in our hearts by the Holy Spirit" (Rom. 5:5). He will also, if need be, provide the opportunity, as He did for me and Mom in Arizona. However, we must be willing to let the hurt go and get on with our lives.

Chapter 13
HOW CAN I FORGIVE?
HOW CAN I FORGET?

I STOPPED TRYING TO figure people out and why they hurt each other a long time ago. The simple truth is that we are humans and humans make mistakes, especially lost sinners who are living without Christ in their lives. When in a state of darkness, people are bound to do things that hurt others. It is part of the sin nature.

Why do people sexually abuse? They are lost in lust and sin. Why doesn't a mother love her child, as she should? Maybe she doesn't understand love or hasn't experienced it in her childhood. Why do men and women commit adultery? They are drawn away by their own lusts. Why does a person lie? Because he is harboring deception in his heart. Explanations of these offenses are varied and could continue ad nauseam, but the root of the problem is simple: it is the power of sin in the flesh of man. In his letter to the Galatians, the apostle Paul talks about the works of the flesh. He provides a list of examples of these works, all of which begin in the heart and flesh of sinful man.

> Now the works of the flesh are evident, which are: adultery, fornication, uncleanness, lewdness [lustfulness],

> idolatry, sorcery, hatred, contentions, jealousies, outbursts
> of wrath, selfish ambitions, dissensions, heresies, envy,
> murders, drunkenness, revelries [rebellion], and the like.
> —Galatians 5:19–21

It is certain that those that walk after the flesh fulfill the lust of the flesh. (See Galatians 5:16.) These people are in darkness (lack wisdom) and do not operate after the will of God, but rather their own natural man's desires. Unfortunately, people who operate in the flesh are bound to hurt others as well as themselves. The flesh profits nothing. (See John 6:63.) If someone has sinned and done terrible things outside of the knowledge of God, it is understandable because they were driven by sin and the powers of darkness. It is obvious; someone who will molest a small child is not walking in light and truth. A person that will lie, cheat, and betray without a thought is not following after the Spirit.

We must try to understand that sin and darkness has taken hold of many. Can we extend a hand of forgiveness and love, even to those that have reviled us and spoken evil against us? Are we able to look at the ones who have betrayed us and see past their behavior to realize that they were in darkness and need to be set free? This is a hard task to commit to in word, but it is even harder to do. Remember that God forgave us. While we were yet sinners, He died for us. "While I was yet;" that is truly amazing grace. Let's learn to extend that same grace to others.

THE FOUNTAIN OF HIS BLOOD WASHES CLEAN

After we are born again, we are instructed not to hurt others and to strive to live a godly life. Betraying others should not be part of our behavior. Unfortunately, even people who know the Lord make mistakes, as did David when he betrayed

Uriah. Samson betrayed his oath and the secret of his power, and Peter betrayed the Lord by swearing he never knew Him. All three of these men, though guilty, repented and found forgiveness in the God of mercy and grace.

God was willing to pay an incredible price for our lives. We have not been bought with things that perish such as silver or gold, but with the precious Blood of a pure and spotless Lamb, Jesus Christ, the Son of God. Both the sinner who walks after the flesh, as well as the Christian who has knowledge of the power of God, can go to the fountain of Christ's cleansing blood and be washed from their sins. The sinner can simply ask God to forgive them and accept Jesus Christ into their heart. Now they can know the love of God and His wonderful plan of salvation. All of this is just too wonderful and marvelous. It makes it clear to us how much God loves the human race and how He is compassionate of our fallen state.

The Bible says that out of our bellies will flow rivers of living waters. (See John 7:38.) These waters are to quench the thirst of a lost and dying world, but for many of us who have been hurt bitterness and resentment block the rivers.

A woman once told me a strange story from her childhood growing up on a farm. On this farm they had what they call an artisan well. It was deep, and the water that came out of it was pure and clean. It came from a stream that ran underground. Every morning before the children woke up, their dad would go out and fill a bucket with water from the well. They would ladle it out and drink. "It was so delicious," she told me. One morning after a fresh bucket was brought in, the children began to drink it, as usual. However, this morning it was putrid. It tasted rotten and it stunk badly. Their dad went out and began to dig around the well to see what the problem was. About three feet down he found a large rat that had fallen in, clogging the pipe. As the water came up from the pure source, it would filter through that lodged rat, making the water unclean at the surface.

Unfortunately, there are some of us who have a rat stuck in our pipes, blocking our wells of living water. It is the rat of bitterness and hatred, and every time that water comes up it picks up the sediment of that lodged rat. Sounds crude, I know, but it made me think about the different things that are lodged in our heart and how they affect our lives. We can keep the hate and its fruit, or forgive and be refreshed.

Chapter 14
STEPS TO RECOVERY

Step one

Admit that you are hurt and you have been betrayed. The feelings of pain, hurt, anger, and distrust are all normal at first.

However, be sure to examine any anger and rage that have grown from the seeds of betrayal. These seeds were watered with years of unforgiveness and fertilized with the stone-cold refusal to face what is in one's heart. I know a minister named Joel who preaches the gospel to men who are in prison. He told me about an experience that he had one afternoon when he laid hands on a young man to pray for him. The man began to tremble violently. Joel then asked him, "What are you feeling, my friend?" The young man continued to shake and answered with clenched teeth, "I feel rage, such terrible rage!" It is possible that this young man had experienced some sort of betrayal and had buried it deep down inside until the power of God came upon him, rooted it up, and forced it out.

If you discover that rage has become part of your personality as a result of having been betrayed, I urge you to get the help you need to be free of it. The power of God is sufficient for deliverance. If you feel you need someone to talk to or walk you through a problem with rage, I strongly suggest you contact your pastor or a counselor.

Step two

In order to be able to forgive someone, we must realize that all have sinned—all! That means me and you and everybody else. We all have to face the truth that at one time or another we have all been guilty of doing someone wrong. Your first response might be, "Yes, but I never did anything that bad to anyone else." Even so, you must tell your heart that in spite of the fact that your feelings may seem justified, you want to forgive and be free of all bitterness and hate.

This is the decision part of your recovery, the part where your will comes in. You must yield your will to the will of God. That will require giving up on carrying around the resentment, whether justified or not.

After one of my regular examinations, my dentist told me that on the surface my teeth were pretty clean, however, he had found tartar down under the gums where the eye can't see. Though it was hidden, it was harboring bacteria that would lead to bone disease, if left untreated. "The thing to do," my dentist said, "is a deep cleaning to get to all the hidden stuff that will cause the disease." Just like that tartar, some of us have hidden things in our hearts. Though they may not be noticeable to the eye, they are causing a disease within us. We have to let God do a deep cleaning in our hearts. This begins by letting the Holy Spirit go deep to where the wound is and clean it out.

Once you have made this decision and are ready to give your will over to the will of God, it is time to pray. Say it out loud: "Lord, I have been hurt by the people that I love. I have been terribly injured, and it has affected my heart. I have anger, bitterness and resentment. I choose to forgive that person or those persons who violated my emotions and my trust."

At this point you release your faith. Don't worry about how much faith you have. The faith of a mustard seed will do. Allow God's supernatural power to fill your heart and assist in the act of forgiving.

Next, believe God for His assistance in relieving the terrible feelings you have. When you are affected by betrayal, these feelings are the baggage that you will carry through life, but they must be dealt with. Pray with sincerity that the Holy Spirit would begin a work in your heart immediately and help you every time the feelings try to rule and rebirth bitterness and anger.

Step three

"Cast your cares on Him, because He cares for you" (1 Peter 5:7, author's paraphrase). Give it to God. Don't try to get even or to repay with revenge. Don't repay evil for evil. Don't curse them that have despitefully used you. Be determined to let go and let God. Simply open the door for God's blessings in your life by choosing to love your enemies. This will be a struggle, but it's better than feeling the hate, resentment, bitterness, and anger. Now that you have admitted to the betrayal and have chosen to forgive the one who wounded you, you will experience a feeling of release and refreshment. Now God can begin a healing in your heart and mind.

Step four

Begin to pray that the Holy Spirit will strengthen you in your inner man. Believe that "He who has begun a good work in you will complete it until the day of Jesus Christ" (Phil. 1:6). Remember that God's power is working inside of you to do His good pleasure!

Do not be hesitant to ask faithful people to pray for you concerning any lingering memories. I can tell you from experience that everything you pray for, with time and diligence applied, will come to pass. He who has promised is faithful!

Chapter 15
REGRET: TO FEEL SORRY
ABOUT SOMETHING

I HAVE OFTEN SAID that regret is one of the saddest words in the dictionary. As I said earlier, I have experienced firsthand the regret and terrible remorse that one feels after betraying someone that loves you and trusts you. Once I was able to acknowledge that I had done someone wrong, I knew that I had to repent with a true repentance. This requires a total turn around and a commitment not to do it again.

Yes, the Lord is faithful and He will forgive us because He is full of mercy, but once the dye is cast we have to face the repercussions of our mistakes. However, some people are very limited when it comes to mercy, and we must try to understand their feelings. If we betrayed them, then what we did to them was wrong. They have a right to be hurt. We must accept in our hearts that the mistake of betraying them is on our part. They may need time and space to even begin to deal with it, or they may choose never to forgive us. Whatever the case, we must remain determined to walk in love toward them.

Good Guilt and Bad Guilt

I had to decide if it would be appropriate to go to the person and ask their forgiveness, but in my case this was not possible. I had to deal with the feeling of regret. There were times when I felt like I couldn't rest because the person that I had betrayed had not heard my heart-felt apology. I allowed regret to take up residence in my heart. I was convinced that I would never be free of it, but God has changed that.

I have learned that guilt that eats away at an individual is not from God. There is a bad guilt and a good guilt. Let me explain.

When we do something wrong and our conscience begins to bother us, guilt comes. This "good guilt" points us to the need to recognize that we have done wrong, and that we should repent and make it right. Once we have put forth a sincere effort and have repented, guilt should be erased. This is not to say that occasionally what we have done won't come to mind, causing us to feel a bit of that guilt again. However, when the guilt eats at us, condemns us, confuses us, and finally depresses us, this type of "bad guilt" is unhealthy and comes from the devil.

Now when I reflect back on the mistakes I have made and the people I have betrayed, I feel regretful, but I refuse to live in condemnation and guilt. Jesus Christ has made provision for my weaknesses by His blood. Once I have confessed my sins, "He is faithful and just to forgive us our sins, and to cleanse us from all unrighteousness" (1 John 1:9).

Don't Look Back

It is important to go on with our lives, having learned from our mistakes. We need to be very careful not to repeat the pattern. Before we walk into sin we must take into consideration the fact that friendships are valuable and marriage is scared. If we are in partnership, we should strive to be trustworthy. People often say, "I fell into sin." But the truth is that you didn't fall into that sin, my friend. You dug that pit with a teaspoon! The Bible states that with every temptation God makes a way out for us. (See 1 Corinthians 10:13.)

How does one get on with their life and live with the fact that they have hurt innocent people? Or how can one who has been hurt truly get over it? God is so full of grace, a grace that has brought salvation to the whole world. What is also wonderful is that if we make mistakes, the Lord forgives us, even when men and women won't.

The Apostle Paul knew this secret. I often wondered how a man who had persecuted the church and put innocent people in to prison for worshiping the Lord he now served could say he had a clear conscience. I know he was truly sorry; he expressed that in his letters. But I often wondered, "How does he live with himself? How does he deal with regret and sorrow for the people he caused so much suffering?" He shared his secret with the church at Philippi, saying, "Brethren, I count not myself to have apprehended: but this one thing I do, forgetting those things which are behind, and reaching forth unto those things which are before, I press toward the mark for the prize of the high calling of God in Christ Jesus" (Phil. 3:13–14, KJV). This must also be our determination. With our will yielded and our position secure in Christ, we can overcome any type of betrayal. His healing balm is available—dear friend, be set free!

NOTES

INTRODUCTION

1. *Webster's New Collegiate Dictionary*, 9th ed., s.v. "betray."

Chapter 6

BETRAYED BY LIES

1. Ibid., s.v. "trust."

TO CONTACT THE AUTHOR

www.carolkornacki.org